ESSENTIAL FLY FISHING

ESSENTIAL

FLY FISHING

TOM MEADE

ILLUSTRATIONS BY
JOHN ROBERT WHITE

THE LYONS PRESS

Printed in Hong Kong
Design by Howard P. Johnson
10 9 8 7 6

Library of Congress Cataloging-in-Publication Data

Meade, Tom, 1947–
     Essential fly fishing / Tom Meade ; illustrated by John Robert White.
          p.   cm.
     Includes bibliographical references and index.
     ISBN 1-55821-334-1
     1. Fly fishing.   I. Title.
SH456.M43   1994
799.1'2—dc20   94-18502
                                                                                      CIP

Front matter illustrations:

pp. xii–xiii: "Liquid Sunshine"—Autumn Fishing

pp. xiv–xv: "Afternoon Showers"—Grand River, Alaska

pp. xvi–xvii: "Matching The Hatch"

To Marie

CONTENTS

FOREWORD

When I began to fly fish more than forty years ago, I found the entire sport bewildering in the extreme. I began by threading my fly line through the hook-keeper ring; I progressed by having to string line through the guides five times because it kept slipping back through. I taught myself to cast and promptly developed a dozen habits that later took me years to undo; I acted clownishly on the stream because I didn't know "the rules of the game"; I mismatched the hatches, tied knots that never held, fell in, carried far too much gear and then far too little, and missed every good fish I pursued.

It was more difficult than work and less than fun.

I was several times convinced that it was all quite impossible; that I should return to bait and spinning; that fly fishing was far more complex than I'd assumed and not nearly as pleasurable. It was often billed as elitist, affected, and wrapped in mystery.

How I wish I'd had a good crisp primer like *Essential Fly Fishing* then. It would have saved me from huge errors; it would have made my transition from other kinds of fishing much more comfortable; it would have given me the base, the firm and practical foundation, from which to move off in my own idiosyncratic way to the advanced levels that give me such immense joy, satisfaction, and the sense of engaging in an activity you can never fully enjoy until you've mastered somewhat, but will never master entirely.

Tom Meade has taken nothing for granted; he has written a book that gently leads the interested beginner through the diverse group of skills he must learn before fly fishing can provide very much pleasure at all: casting, reading the water, understanding what the fly imitates and how to manipulate it in the water or let it move downstream "dead drift," understanding your quary and tackle, and matching rods, reels, and lines to different gamefish. He offers a patient short course on the ethics of fly fishing, proper relationships to other anglers on the water or to guides. And he presents a sound and annotated list of several dozen books, with which any starting fly fisher can enter the wider world of angling literature and more sophisticated and specialized techniques.

There are other fine fly fishing primers—and no doubt there will be more. But Tom Meade's *Essential Fly Fishing*, with the handsome color paintings by Bob White illustrating the text, will prove an invaluable aid to people who want to enter the magical, enduring world of fly fishing.

I wish I'd had it when I stumbled into this sport that has given me such immense pleasure for my whole adult life.

—Nick Lyons

PREFACE

> **"**Once a journey is designed, equipped, and
> put in process, a new factor emerges and takes
> over. A trip, a safari, an exploration,
> is an entity different from all other
> journeys. It has a personality, temperament,
> individuality, uniqueness. A journey is a
> person in itself; no two are alike. And all
> plans, safeguards, policing, and coercion are
> fruitless. We find after years of struggle that
> we do not take a trip; a trip takes us.**"**
>
> **—JOHN STEINBECK**
> Travels with Charlie

You are about to start a lifetime trip to a world of discovery. Through fly fishing, you will learn to see creatures invisible to other people. You will discover a new world of literature, new friends, new places—far flung and near at hand, and all interesting.

The fly rod is an extraordinary fishing tool, enabling you to catch fish when other anglers cannot. Once you learn the rhythm of the rod, however, simply fishing with it may become more gratifying than catching with it. The rhythm of the rod carries your body, mind, and spirit to the water. Whether you catch a fish or not, the water will always give you a little of its strength, some of its energy, and much of its peace. As you fall asleep after a day of fly fishing, you can feel the rhythm of the rod and of the water.

Fly fishing is paradoxical: It will stimulate you as it relaxes you. It is as simple or as complex as you want it to be.

Learning to fish with a fly rod is easy, even though it may not seem so at first. Casting requires neither strength nor genius. It helps to have a little rhythm and some coordination; if you can tap your fingers to a tune, that's enough.

You can master the fundamentals of fly fishing in a weekend, and you can spend a lifetime learning about the sport, the art, and the science of fly fishing from hundreds of wonderful books and videotapes, and from the new friends you're going to meet. Your best teachers will be the water—its currents and creatures.

When we worked together on *Fly Fisherman* Magazine, John Randolph, my editor and friend, would say that there was nothing new in fly fishing, only variations on proven tackle and techniques. So it is with this handbook: It contains an assortment of proven teaching techniques

from five fly-fishing schools, dozens of workshops and seminars, and scores of brilliant authors. The book contains ideas collected by a student on a Maryland pond with Lefty Kreh, on a casting pool with Harry Scott, and on the water with Cathy and Barry Beck, Bob Clouser, Ken Miyata, Steve Rajeff, Ed Shenk, Sharon and Chuck Tryon, and many other expert anglers, generous with their knowledge. It contains ideas from conversations with Fred Arbona, Gary Borger, Frank Daignault, Jack Dennis, Jack Gartside, Joe Humphreys, Ed Jaworowski, Eric Leiser, Ed Leonard, Nick Lyons, Tom Rosenbauer, Lou Tabory, and John Voelker, all of whom have written bright and important books you should read as you become more involved in fly fishing and fly tying. Many ideas came from John Robert White, whose paintings and illustrations grace this book. During the summer in Alaska, Bob is a professional fishing guide; in a morning of on-stream instruction, he can turn a rank novice into a respectable fly fisher.

This is a book of suggestions, not dogma. Because each of us responds to different ideas, the book sometimes suggests several ways to accomplish a single goal. Usually, one of those suggestions clicks. In the chapter on casting, for instance, you will find several ideas for developing the rhythm of the cast. If one suggestion works for you, stick with it and skim the others until it's time to start another subject. If one suggestion doesn't work, try another, and refer to Bob White's illustrations to reinforce ideas.

The most fundamental element of fly fishing is observation. If you are a curious person, you are going to love fly fishing. There is so much to see, to hear, to smell and to feel in the water. When fly fishing becomes a lifelong journey, your senses will become much keener, and you will experience another world.

Welcome aboard.

THE RIGHT TACKLE

"*If undressed and put back on the shelf piece by piece the financier would have stocked a sporting goods store. Placed end to end his collection of flies would have reached from Keokuk, Illinois to Paris, Ontario. The price of his rod would have made a substantial dent in the interallied debt or served to foment a Central American revolution.***"**

—ERNEST HEMINGWAY
Byline: Ernest Hemingway

For some fly fishers, shopping for fly-fishing gear is almost as much fun as fishing itself, especially during the winter. When the first fishing-tackle catalog of the season appears, it brings dreams of spring.

Selecting the right fly-fishing gear to start is easy when you buy from a fly-fishing outfitter who offers personal advice, sets up your gear, and assures your satisfaction with a reasonable return policy.

Before you begin, decide what kind of fishing you're going to do. To learn about the best fishing opportunities near your home, ask other anglers, check the fishing column in your newspaper, or talk to your local fly-fishing dealer.

When you know what kind of fish you're going to pursue, you will have an idea about the kinds of flies you will need and the kind of gear to buy so your entire outfit is matched, or "balanced."

Fishing for trout and sunfish, for example, generally requires small flies that look like insects or small baitfish. The fly weighs almost nothing, and it is connected to a weightless leader, a length of clear line invisible to the fish. At the other end of the leader, a fly line—weighted in front—carries the fly and leader to the fish.

For most trout fishing, a fairly lightweight and easy-to-cast fly rod propels the line. During a cast, your hand and arm accelerate to make the rod bend and load with energy. When you stop the rod suddenly, it releases the energy into the fly line and propels it, with the leader and fly, to the water.

Flies that catch bass and saltwater fish are much larger than trout flies, and require heavier lines and more powerful rods to cast them.

Getting started in fly fishing is not expensive. Most fly-fishing outfitters sell budget-priced starter kits containing everything you will need except a cap, sunglasses, and some flies.

Eventually, you may fill a closet with tackle including . . .

FLIES
•••••••

The challenge of fly fishing is to make fish strike dressed-up hooks that appear to be living creatures. Your fly boxes will contain many kinds of flies, designed for a variety of functions.

DRY FLIES float and simulate insects on the water's surface to lure trout, bass, and many other kinds of fish. Dry flies generally have stiff and oily rooster feathers wound around them to keep them afloat.

Dry flies: Artificial and natural mayfly (top) and caddisfly (bottom).

WET FLIES sink for fishing beneath the water's surface. They usually simulate water-born insects swimming to the surface to emerge as adults before they fly away.

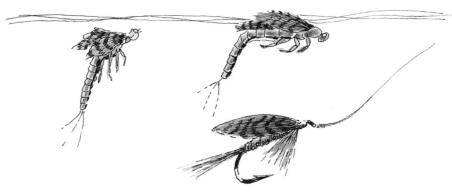

Wet flies: Natural emerging nymphs (top) and artificial nymph (bottom).

NYMPHS, LARVAE, AND PUPAE Generally fished near the bottom, these flies look like the immature aquatic insects that comprise a large part of a freshwater fish's diet.

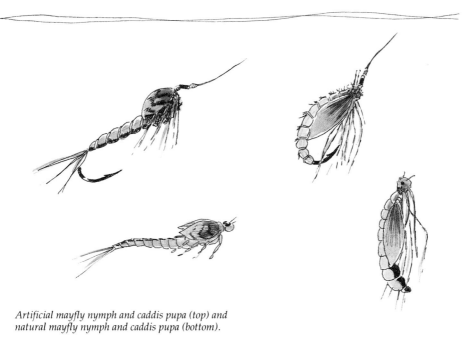

Artificial mayfly nymph and caddis pupa (top) and natural mayfly nymph and caddis pupa (bottom).

Streamer (top) and natural minnow (bottom).

STREAMERS Long, sinking flies that usually simulate fish, streamers lure strikes because they behave like prey, and sometimes like predators about to invade a gamefish's territory. Streamers also may represent leeches, snakes, and other large creatures that fish eat.

Bass bug (left) and natural frog (right).

BASS BUGS Made of cork, deer hair, and other buoyant materials, bass bugs are crafted to look like frogs, mice, and other creatures in a bass' diet. Some simulate huge insects such as dragonflies, and others look like nothing at all in nature, but predatory fish attack them anyway.

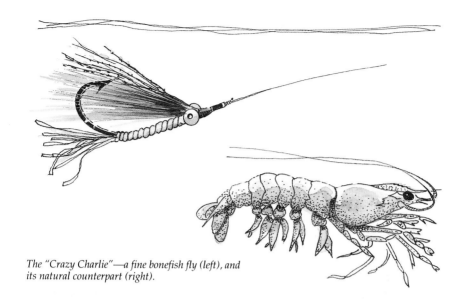

The "Crazy Charlie"—a fine bonefish fly (left), and
its natural counterpart (right).

SALTWATER FLIES Shrimp, crabs, and eels are among the many animals fly crafters replicate with artificial flies. Most saltwater flies, however, are designed to imitate baitfish.

Fly fishers use numbers to indicate the size of flies. They range from #32, so tiny that several of them will fit on an adult's thumbnail, to saltwater fish imitations as long as your foot.

The higher the number used to describe the size of a fly, the smaller the fly.

The chapter on what fish eat and the lists of recommended flies at the back of this book will help you select the most effective flies for the kind of fish you plan to catch. Also, ask your fly-fishing outfitter and other anglers for advice about which flies to use.

MAKING A POINT

Whether you buy flies or make them yourself, always pinch down the barb of the hook with a pair of needle-nose pliers, and sharpen the point with a diamond hook sharpener.

Run the hook point lightly over your thumbnail; if the point sticks, it's sharp.

Sharpened and barbless, artificial flies will hook more fish for you. Barbless hooks also are easy to remove when you release a fish or when you hook yourself accidentally.

LEADERS AND TIPPETS

After selecting the right fly to catch fish, you must use the correct leader, the connection between the fly and the fly line. Leaders for most fly-fishing applications are virtually weightless, transparent, and tapered from a thick "butt" section to a thin point, or "tippet."

The thick butt connects to the end of the fly line. The leader receives energy from the line during the cast to propel the fly toward its target.

The fly is tied to the tippet, which is very thin so that fish do not notice it: A wary fish is as suspicious of flies attached to heavy line as you would be about a sandwich attached to a rope. When you are certain that you are fishing the correct fly, but fish refuse to strike it, your tippet may be too thick.

When you change flies, you cut off some of the tippet end, shortening the leader. However, several fishing-line makers produce spools of replacement tippet material so you can restore the leader to its original length—or lengthen it. With new tippets, a single leader may last for an entire fishing season.

Leaders come in three basic models: "braided," "compound," and "knotless."

Braided leaders are more popular in Europe than in America, where they fall in and out of fashion. The thick butt section is made of braided line that, some anglers believe, is easier to cast than a solid strand.

Compound leaders use several strands of translucent fishing line of different thickness, tied together to make the whole leader taper from the thick butt end to the thin tippet. Advocates of compound leaders believe that the leader's construction makes floating artificial flies behave more like natural insects on the water. The sections of thin line leading to the tippet help prevent "drag"—which occurs when water currents make an artificial fly act unnaturally.

A knotless leader is a single strand of material, drawn through a machine that makes it thick at the butt end and thin at the tippet end. You can make the thin end even thinner by tying on a length

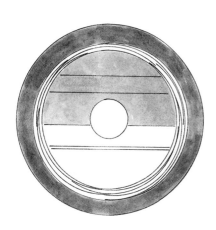

Tippet spool

mid-section   tip   tippet

Leader tapers: Hand-tied knotted leader (top) and tapered knotless leader with tippet (bottom).

of finer tippet line. Knotless leaders are especially convenient when fishing weedy water because there are no knots to hang up in the weeds.

When you are fishing streamer flies beneath the water's surface, you can use a leader shorter than six feet; a two-footer often is long enough.

For fishing flies on the water's surface or just beneath it, you will need leaders of standard length, from seven and one-half to twelve feet long. Shorter leaders are easier to cast, but wary fish and crystalline water usually require smaller flies, longer leaders, and finer tippets.

Fishing-line companies describe tippet thickness in X-numbers, from 0X to 8X. *The higher the X-number, the thinner the tippet and the smaller the fly it will cast.* For example, tippets measuring 6X, 7X, and 8X are used on the most minuscule flies. Tippets measuring 2X, 1X and OX are used for large bass bugs and some steelhead and saltwater flies.

A simple way to select an appropriate tippet for a particular fly is to take the size of the fly and divide it by three. For example, on a medium-sized #12 fly, a 4X tippet would be ideal. Dividing a tiny #22 fly by three, the closest tippet size is 7X.

"Shock tippets" or "bite tippets" are made of wire or other materials that resist abrasion from such fish as northern pike and bluefish, which have extremely sharp teeth that can chop off standard leaders.

Fly with serpentine tippet on the surface of the water.

FLY LINE

Tackle manufacturers design fly lines and matching fly rods for specific fishing situations. *Generally, the larger the fish you plan to catch, the larger the fly you will cast, and the heavier the line weight you will need.* You can, however, catch very large fish on very light fly tackle, and small fish sometimes strike large flies cast on heavy gear.

For fishing tiny flies with finesse, many advanced fly fishers use 1-, 2-, or 3-weight lines. Most trout anglers prefer 4- to 7-weight fly lines. For bass, pike, and light saltwater fishing, 7- to 10-weight lines are ideal, and 11-, 12- and 13-weight lines are made for big-game fishing. If you had to choose a single all-purpose fly line, a 7-weight would be a good bet.

Once you have decided on the line weight to suit the kind of fishing you're going to do, it is time to select the best "taper" and buoyancy for your fishing.

The front end of a fly line is thin at its tip so the fly and leader will fall gently to the water at the end of a cast. The line quickly becomes thicker, or tapers into the "belly" section, providing the weight that allows the rod to throw the line. Then the line tapers down to a long, narrow section of "running line."

Some lines contain air bubbles that make them float. Other lines are so dense they sink. High-density lines sink faster than low-density models.

The taper, line weight, and buoyancy appear on the end of a fly-line box. A box of fly line for trout fishing, for instance, may say "WF 5 F" which means "weight-forward (the taper), 5-weight, floating." Here's what the line-box terms mean:

DOUBLE-TAPER (DT)   The line is thin at both ends and then gets thicker toward the middle. Instead of narrowing into a thin running line, it remains fairly thick in the middle. When you learn the roll cast or a maneuver called mending, a double-taper line makes them easy. Also, because both ends of the line are identical, you can reverse the ends when one wears out, doubling the life of your line.

WEIGHT-FORWARD   The most popular line, it is thin at the leader end, and it tapers to a thick belly about six feet long. Then the line quickly tapers into a thin running line that makes it easier to cast for distance. *For most freshwater fishing, a weight-forward fly line is the easiest to use.*

SPECIALTY TAPERS   More fly-line makers are designing lines for specific types of fish such as bass, bonefish, and tarpon. Such lines generally have short, thick bellies for quick, long casts.

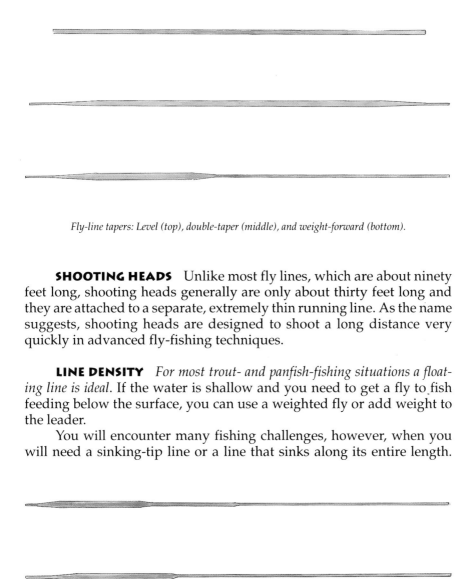

Fly-line tapers: Level (top), double-taper (middle), and weight-forward (bottom).

SHOOTING HEADS Unlike most fly lines, which are about ninety feet long, shooting heads generally are only about thirty feet long and they are attached to a separate, extremely thin running line. As the name suggests, shooting heads are designed to shoot a long distance very quickly in advanced fly-fishing techniques.

LINE DENSITY *For most trout- and panfish-fishing situations a floating line is ideal.* If the water is shallow and you need to get a fly to fish feeding below the surface, you can use a weighted fly or add weight to the leader.

You will encounter many fishing challenges, however, when you will need a sinking-tip line or a line that sinks along its entire length.

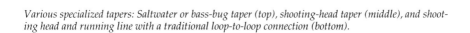

Loop-to-loop connection

Various specialized tapers: Saltwater or bass-bug taper (top), shooting-head taper (middle), and shooting head and running line with a traditional loop-to-loop connection (bottom).

On a sinking-tip line, only the front of the line sinks and the rest floats, making it easier to start a cast. Sinking-tip fly lines are available in high-density models that sink quickly—ideal for fishing in fast-flowing water—and lower-density versions that sink slowly for fishing a fly in shallow water. To work a fly in very deep water, select a full-sinking line, which goes to the bottom along the line's entire length.

Fly-line companies also make a versatile line labeled "intermediate": When you coat it with a water-repellent substance such as silicone, an intermediate line floats. Without such a coating, the line sinks very slowly. An intermediate line is good for fishing flies just beneath the water's surface.

If you can afford to splurge on only one item of tackle, ask your fly-fishing outfitter for the best fly line your budget can handle. A top-quality weight-forward floating line is the best for a starter.

Most fly lines will last for several seasons if you keep them clean, wash them occasionally with a gentle liquid soap, and do not store them in sunlight. Keep sunscreen solutions and insect repellents away from fly lines because the chemicals eat into the line's surface.

BACKING Made of a supple braided material, backing connects the fly line to the reel, and it keeps you connected to a hooked fish that swims beyond the length of the fly line. Backing also fills the reel spool and provides a cushion that keeps kinks out of the fly line when the line rests on the reel spool for a long time.

FLY RODS

Fly fishers use the term "balanced" to describe an outfit in which each component matches the others, from the fly to the rod and reel.

Tackle manufacturers make each fly rod to cast a particular size line, from 1-weight for ultra-delicate fishing to 13-weight for big-game fishing. Just above a rod's cork handle, or "grip," they list the rod's recommended line weight, length, and actual weight in ounces.

An eight-and-one-half- or nine-foot-long rod will handle most fishing situations. If you are fishing tight little streams with overgrown banks, you may need a shorter rod. For surf fishing and other big-water angling, consider buying a rod longer than nine feet.

Rod butt showing manufacturer's information. This rod, 8' 6" in length and designed to use a #7 fly line, will work well in most *fishing situations.*

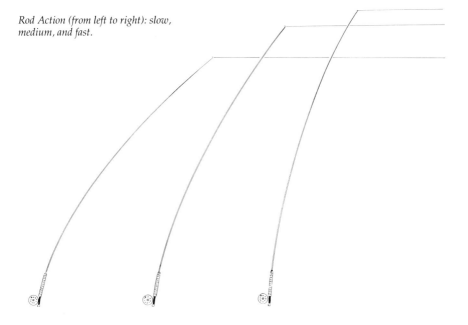

Rod Action (from left to right): slow, medium, and fast.

Fly-fishing outfitters may refer to a rod's "action," describing it in such terms as "fast," "moderate," or "medium," and sometimes as "slow" or "parabolic." The terms describe how and where a rod bends as you cast it.

A fast-action rod is relatively stiff for much of its length and it bends near the top. It generally casts a fly line farther, but it is more difficult for a beginning caster to handle. A moderate- or medium-action rod bends more; it will compensate for many casting errors and generally is easier to fish. Slow- or parabolic-action rods bend along most of their length; they are accurate, but do not cast very far.

Most fly rods come apart in sections so you can stow them easily while you travel. Four-piece rods—ideal for airplane travel—pack down into smaller packages than two-piece fly rods.

The joint connecting one section to another is called a ferrule. On some fly rods, the ferrules fit snugly, but the outer tubes do not come together completely: That's all right. The rod maker designed the ferrule that way so it will remain snug as the joint wears.

When you assemble a fly rod, align the metal loops, called "line guides"; the fly line passes through them from the reel to the tip-top guide at the rod's tip. The tiny ring or piece of metal just above the cork is a hook keeper to hold your fly in place when you're not fishing. Please do not thread your fly line through it.

Beneath the cork grip is the reel seat where you lock on the fly reel with a threaded ring or sliding bands.

One final word about selecting a fly rod: Most manufacturers build the cork grip for an average-size hand. If you have very small hands, an average-size grip may tire your fingers. Look for a grip that feels comfortable; if you cannot find one, a sheet of sandpaper will reduce the thickness of the cork.

FLY REELS

A fly reel is more than a device to store line. When you hook a large fish, your rod will help you fight it, and your reel will help keep you from losing it.

The most important part of a reel, the "drag," is inside beneath the spool. The drag mechanism works like a car's brakes: It reduces the speed of a spinning spool and puts pressure on a hooked fish trying to escape. It should be strong enough to convince a fish that you are in charge, and smooth enough to prevent the fish from breaking off. Reels with jerky drags cause leaders to snap.

Besides tightening the internal drag, you can also use the rim of a fly-reel spool to put additional pressure on a hooked fish. The technique is called "palming" because you apply pressure to the spool's rim with the palm of one hand as you hold the rod with your other hand. Palming is an effective fish-fighting technique but you must be

WE STINK

As far as a fish is concerned, humans—particularly males—stink.

The skin of many men and boys contains a substance that smells repulsive to fish. In British Columbia, some professional fishing guides use lemon-scented dish-washing detergent to remove the human smell from flies and lures. In the United States, several companies make solutions that either eliminate or mask human scent. Using one of the biodegradable solutions before you start fishing is probably a good idea.

If you prefer to remain completely natural, consider rubbing the mud from a streambank on your hands before you start fishing. Rubbing mud into an artificial fly not only makes it smell more natural, but also makes it sink faster. Applying fish attractants or crushed bait to a fly, however, is generally regarded as unethical.

careful of the reel's handle on a "direct-drive" or "single-action" reel; as the fish tears line off the reel, the spool spins and the handle can bruise your fingers.

On an "anti-reverse" reel, the handle does not spin as the fish tries to escape. Anti-reverse models cost more than direct-drive reels, but they are valuable tools for fighting salmon and other big gamefish.

Most reels come with the handle placed for a fisher who cranks with the right hand, an old but inefficient tradition. If you are right-handed, it is easier to hold the rod in that hand and to wind with your left; select a fly reel made for left-hand cranking or a model that is reversible.

Most of today's fly reels resist corrosion as long as you keep them clean and well lubricated with a special grease available at fly-fishing stores.

OTHER ESSENTIALS

To start fishing, you need only two other pieces of gear: a pair of polarized sunglasses and a cap with a brim long enough to shade your eyes. They will help you find fish and prevent an injury.

When your eyes are shaded, polarized sunglasses cut through the glare on the water's surface so you can spot fish. The cap and glasses also protect your head and eyes from the hook as you cast. When you are fishing at night, please wear clear safety glasses to protect your eyes.

Polarized glasses reduce water-surface glare and protect your eyes and head.

BOOTS AND ACCESSORIES

If you plan to wade in cool water, invest in a good pair of boots. Waders come in three lengths: to the hip, the waist, and the chest.

Stocking-foot waders require a separate pair of wading shoes that provide foot and ankle support, and they are easy to pack. Boot-foot waders have the shoe attached to the bottom; they are quick to put on and the boots keep your feet warm in cold water. Boot-foot waders, however, are bulky to pack.

For most fishing situations, the bottoms of your boots should have non-skid felt soles for walking on slippery rocks, or metal cleats for even more traction.

Wading-boot makers use a variety of materials including light-weight synthetic cloths for warm-weather wading, coated and insulated high-density fabrics to resist abrasion and tearing, and waterproof foam, which is very warm and buoyant.

When you're wearing chest-high waders, please cinch a wading belt around your waist: If you *do* fall in, the belt will keep your boots from flooding.

MORE GEAR

THERMOMETER   Use it often to locate freshwater fish. (See the chapter on where to find fish.)

STRIKE INDICATORS   The fly fisher's version of a bobber, a strike indicator signals fish bites when your fly is beneath the surface.

WADING STAFF   Used as a third leg while wading in fast-flowing water, it will keep you from falling.

FISHING VEST   With plenty of pockets it holds all your tackle, rain gear, and even lunch.

RAIN JACKET   A crushable model is best because you can carry it in your vest.

CHEST- OR FANNY-PACK   Alternatives to a vest, they are ideal for warm-weather fishing or wading in shallow salt water.

NIPPERS   to cut line and trim leaders.

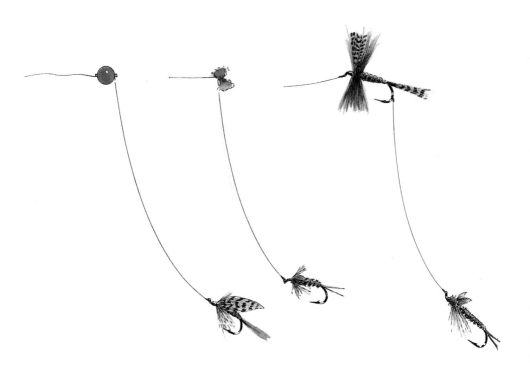

Strike indicators (from left to right): Wet fly using a cork float; nymph us-ing a greased-yarn indicator; emerger with a large attractor dry fly.

THE FLY FISHER'S BOBBER

"Strike indicator" is the fly fisher's term for the device that bait an-glers call a bobber. Though a strike indicator is much smaller and lighter than a bobber, it works the same way, floating on the surface, bobbing or pausing to signal that a fish is biting beneath the surface.

Strike indicators also eliminate drag. Many aquatic insects and worms periodically experience "drift" when the current carries large num-bers of them down the stream and underwater. When a drift occurs, fish start feeding, but they are reluctant to strike anything that is moving un-naturally. A strike indicator on your leader will make imitation nymphs and larvae drift realistically, and it will signal you when a fish bites.

Fly-fishing outfitters sell strike indicators made of hard or soft foam. You also may use a bit of yarn, greased with floatant, on the leader, or even a floating fly to double as a strike indicator and strike attractor.

PLIERS WITH WIRE-CUTTERS to squeeze down hook barbs, and to remove hooks from fish, clothing or skin.

HEMOSTATS to remove hooks from fish.

SAFETY PIN to untangle lines and leaders, remove splinters, and replace buttons that pop.

FIRST AID KIT It doesn't have to be elaborate to be useful.

LANDING NET Helps land fish without fatiguing them unnecessarily.

INSECT NET A tiny net with tight mesh to collect samples of insects so you can match them with artificial flies.

CREEL OR COOLER To keep fresh any fish you plan to eat.

PRIEST A small club to quickly kill fish you plan to eat.

PAPER TOWEL A couple of sheets will dry soggy flies and clean fly line and other gear in the field.

IN A NUTSHELL

1. A fly-fishing outfit is "balanced" with matched components. To cast large flies, you need a heavy fly line with a matching rod. For fishing tiny flies, match a lighter weight rod with a light line and a thin leader.

2. For fishing tiny flies with finesse, many advanced fly fishers use 1-, 2,- or 3-weight lines. Most trout anglers prefer 4- to 7-weight fly lines. For bass, pike, and light saltwater fishing, 7- to 10-weight lines are ideal, and 11-, 12,- and 13-weight lines are made for big-game fishing. If you had to choose a single all-purpose fly line, a 7-weight would be a good bet.

3. A floating, weight-forward fly line will meet most of your fishing needs.

4. Dry flies float. Wet flies sink. Nymphs simulate immature insects and usually are fished near the bottom. Streamers generally represent baitfish.

2

GEARING UP FOR FISHING

> **❝**It is just about time for the solemn trout
> fisherman to start the long spring ceremony
> of getting his tackle in shape for the coming
> season. There are several sound and detailed
> systems for doing this, but by far the best is to
> play helpless. Anybody can do this who has
> suckered a neighbor or friend into showing
> him how to put up storm windows.**❞**
>
> **—JOHN W. RANDOLPH**
> The World of "Wood, Field and Stream"

If you bought your tackle from a fly-fishing store, the outfitter probably spooled your reel with backing, fly line, and possibly a leader connection. If not, you can do it easily by yourself with two knots. The appendix at the back of the book contains illustrations for more knots, but for most fishing you will need only two, the Duncan Loop and the Surgeon's Knot.

Use the Duncan Loop to attach the backing to the reel, the fly line to the backing, and the fly to the tippet. Use the Surgeon's Knot to connect the tippet to the leader.

THE DUNCAN LOOP

To practice tying the knots, use heavy monofilament fishing line, between ten- and twelve-pound test. Because you will use the Duncan Loop most often to tie on flies, practice it often. Start with a large fly and plenty of line, and refer to the illustrations.

The instructions are for a right-hander, so reverse them if you are left-handed.

1. Hold the fly in your left hand. With your right hand insert the end of the line down through the hook eye. That end of the line is the working end. Draw about eight inches of it through the eye, and bring it back against the rest of the line.

2. With your left thumb and index finger, pinch the doubled line together about an inch in front of the fly. With your right hand, take the working end and loop it down and back toward the fly, beneath the rest of the line. The loop is about the size of a silver dollar.

3. The working end of the line is facing right. Place the middle fingers of both hands inside the loop to keep it open.

4. With your right thumb and index finger, wrap the working end through the loop five times toward the right.

5. Remove your middle fingers from the loop and grasp the working end and the rest of the line with your right thumb and index finger. Moisten the line wraps with saliva so they will slide together easily.

6. With your left hand, grasp the fly and pull it toward the left to begin drawing the knot tight.

7. To finish the knot, pull the fly smoothly toward the left and the working end of the line to the right. You may have to use your left thumbnail to close the wraps together, forming a compact knot. When you have tightened it, hold the rest of the leader in your right hand and slide the knot to the eye of the hook.

Tying the Duncan Loop: Begin by holding the fly in your left hand and inserting the working end of the tippet with your right hand through the hook eye.

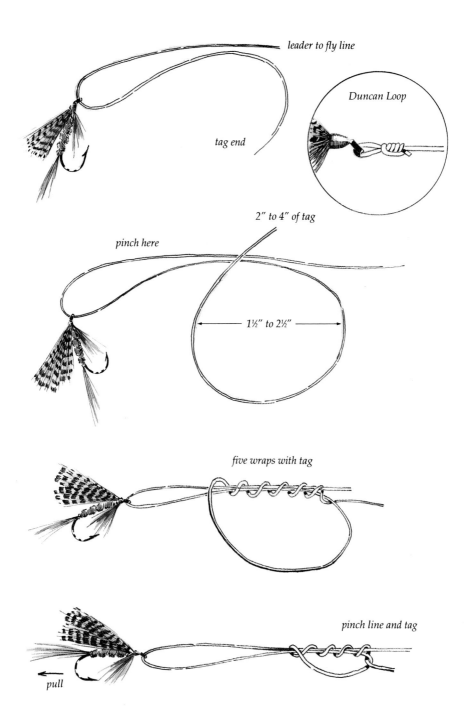

leader to fly line

Duncan Loop

tag end

2" to 4" of tag

pinch here

1½" to 2½"

five wraps with tag

pinch line and tag

pull

Pinch the line together and then create a loop; wrap the working end through the loop five times toward the right; pull the fly smoothly to the left and the line to the right, to tighten the knot.

A loose loop (top) allows additional fly action and helps prevent breaks during hard strikes. A small loop (middle) allows some movement of the fly. A snugged-down knot (bottom) holds the fly tightly and prohibits additional movement.

When you are fishing flies beneath the water's surface, keep the loop open slightly so the fly can "swim" naturally. When a fish strikes and you pull against it, the loop will tighten itself against the hook eye.

Trim away the excess working end, leaving a tiny tip of line next to the knot.

Please follow the illustrations and practice tying the Duncan Loop several times before you move on. Be generous with the amount of line you use on the working end, and remember always to lubricate the line with saliva so the wraps slide together easily.

FILLING YOUR FLY REEL

If you bought all your gear as separate components from an outfitter who did not assemble them for you, it's time to put everything together, starting with the reel. You have to attach the backing line to the reel and wind it on, then connect the fly line to the backing and wind it on, and finally, tie a leader to the end of the fly line. The leader is the nearly invisible connection between the fly line and the fly. Please refer to the illustrations as you read the directions.

Take the end of the backing line, thread it through the wide opening on top of the reel, around the core of the spool, and back out.

Follow the directions for tying the Duncan Loop, above, but use a lot more backing line on the working end, and don't worry about having to hold onto the reel. Put it in your lap or on the table next to you.

When you reach step 5, and you're ready to draw the knot tight, you do not have to moisten the backing line with saliva. Instead, use the fingers of your left hand to manipulate the wraps of backing line together as you draw the knot tight.

When you have completed the knot, trim off the excess working end and use your fingertips to slide the knot tight against the core of the reel spool.

Check the manual that came with the reel to determine how much backing line to wind on. Poke a pencil through the center of the backing-line's spool and crank it onto the reel. For a right-hander, cranking with the left hand generally is easier; crank counterclockwise. A left-handed fisher cranks clockwise with the right hand.

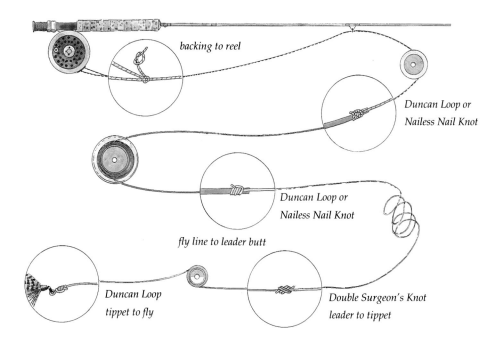

Filling your fly reel (from reel to fly): backing to reel; fly line to backing; leader to fly line; tippet to leader; and fly to tippet. (Refer to instructions in text.)

TYING THE BACKING LINE
TO THE FLY LINE

Use the Duncan Loop again to connect the backing line to the fly line. Most fly-line companies mark the rear of the fly line—the end that connects to the backing—with a tag. Pull about two feet of the fly line off the spool with the tip pointing to the left. Use about ten inches of the backing line as your working end, pointing toward the right.

1. Hold both pieces of line together with your left hand. The end of the fly line is pointing to the left and the backing line is pointing to the right.

2. Bring the working end of the backing line down and back to your left hand to make a loop beneath the lines, and pinch the loop against the fly line. Use your middle fingers to hold the loop open.

3. With your right thumb and index finger, wrap the working end of the backing line toward the right over the fly line and through the loop five times. Pinch each wrap with your left thumb and forefinger.

4. Remove your middle fingers from the loop, grasp both ends of the backing line, and gently pull them away from one another. This time, you don't have to use saliva to lubricate the knot. As you pull, the wraps will close together on the fly line. Don't pull too tightly. Pull a little, then push the wraps together with your thumbnails. Pull a little more and push the wraps tighter with your thumbnails. Continue tightening slowly until you have a compact knot. Test it with a sharp tug.

5. Cut off the excess pieces of fly line and backing line close to the knot.

Now you can crank the fly line onto the reel. It should fill the spool to within three eighths of an inch of the rim. If the spool is so full that the line prevents the reel from turning—it happens to even experienced anglers—you have to pull all the fly line off the spool and remove some backing.

TYING THE LEADER TO THE FLY LINE

The leader is the nearly invisible connection between the fly line and the fly. You can use the Duncan Loop again. Simply follow the directions for tying the backing line to the fly line. Have the end of the fly line pointing to the left and the thick end of the leader pointing to the right.

As you prepare to tighten the knot, lubricate it with saliva and work slowly and gently to tighten the wraps into a compact knot. Test it with a sharp tug.

ATTACHING A NEW TIPPET
TO YOUR LEADER

Eventually, you will have to attach a new tippet to your leader. The tippet that came with the leader may break off on a snag or a fish. It may wear out or be too short after you have changed flies. Or, you may need a thinner piece of line next to the fly because fish appear to be shying away.

Use the Surgeon's Knot: it is easy to tie and strong. Simply, it is a double Overhand Knot. Here are the details:

1. Cut a three-foot-long piece of tippet line off its spool.

2. Overlap about six inches of the thin end of the leader with about six inches of tippet line. The working end of the leader points to the right, and the short end of the tippet line points to the right. Moisten the overlapping lines with saliva so they stick to one another.

3. Pinching the lines together with your left thumb and forefinger, use your right hand to make a simple overhand knot with both pieces of line. Be certain to pass the long end of the tippet line through the loop along with the working end of the leader.

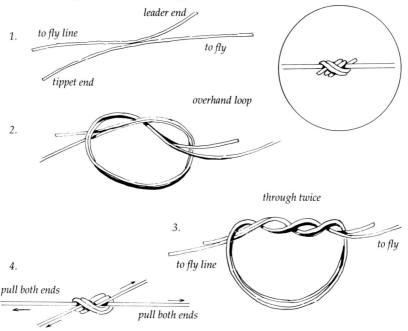

Tying the Double Surgeon's Knot: Overlapping 6 inches of leader and tippet, make two consecutive overhand knots. To tighten the knot, tug at the four individual lines.

4. Before tightening the loop, make another overhand knot with both pieces of line.

5. Grasp all four pieces of line, two in your left hand and two in your right. Moisten them again with saliva, and simultaneously draw all four lengths apart so the wraps slide together in a compact knot.

6. Tug at the individual pieces of line to be certain the knot is tight, and trim away the excess ends close to the knot.

OTHER IMPORTANT KNOTS FOR FLY FISHERS

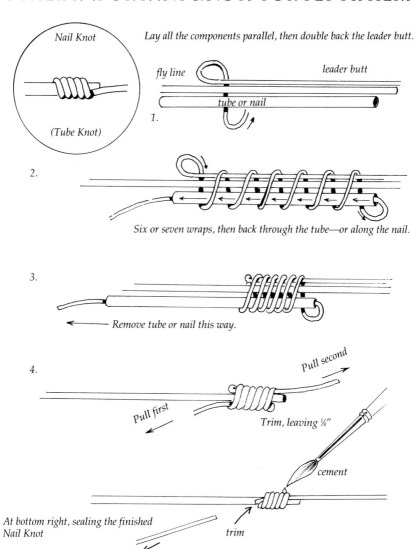

Nail Knot

(Tube Knot)

Lay all the components parallel, then double back the leader butt.

fly line   leader butt

tube or nail

1.

2.

Six or seven wraps, then back through the tube—or along the nail.

3.

Remove tube or nail this way.

4.

Pull second

Pull first

Trim, leaving ⅛"

cement

At bottom right, sealing the finished Nail Knot

trim

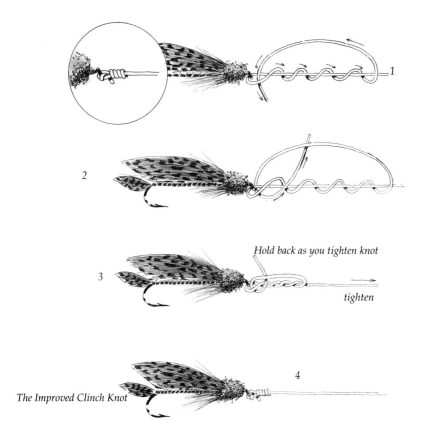

1

2

3

Hold back as you tighten knot

tighten

4

The Improved Clinch Knot

UNCOILING A NEW LEADER

One of the greatest challenges in fly fishing is uncoiling a new leader right out of the package. Most of them were wound by people who were trout in previous lives, and coiling leaders is their way of getting back at fly fishers.

The easiest way to uncoil a new leader is to slip it carefully out of the package, and insert the thumb, index finger, and middle finger of one hand into the center of the coil. Spread your fingers to hold the inside of the coil.

With your other hand, find the thick end of leader—the butt—and carefully unwrap it off the rest of the coil. When you have it unwrapped, hold the end of the butt section and let the rest of the leader fall to the ground as it uncoils itself.

The key is to start by holding the inside of the new leader with three fingers inside the coil.

The Needle Knot—to start

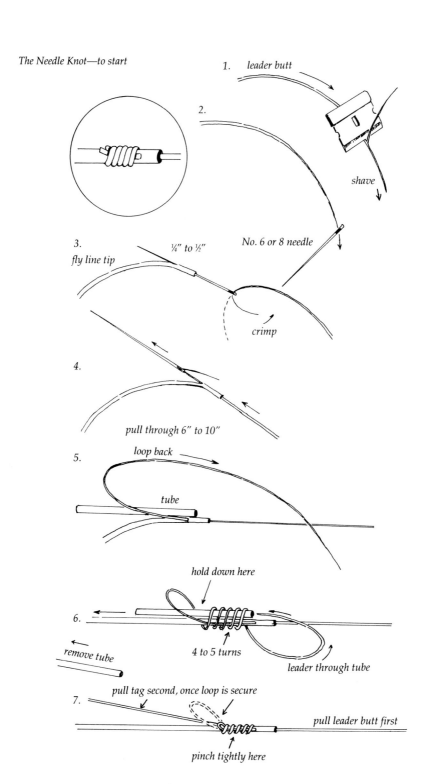

1. *leader butt*

2.

shave

No. 6 or 8 needle

3.
fly line tip ¼" to ½"

crimp

4.

pull through 6" to 10"

5. *loop back*

tube

hold down here

6.

remove tube 4 to 5 turns

leader through tube

7. *pull tag second, once loop is secure*

pull leader butt first

pinch tightly here

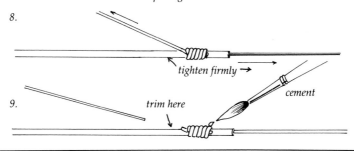

The Needle Knot—
completing the knot

8.

tighten firmly →

9.

trim here

cement

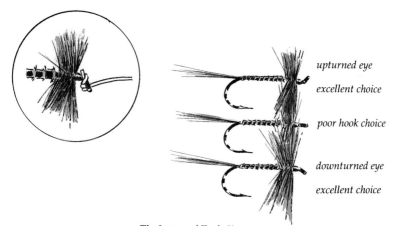

upturned eye

excellent choice

poor hook choice

downturned eye

excellent choice

The Improved Turle Knot—
and proper choice of hook

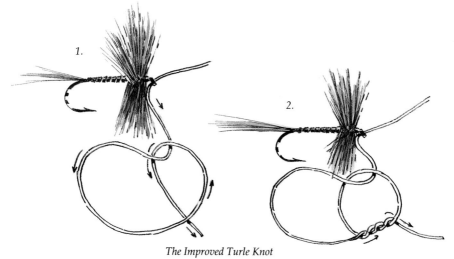

1.

2.

The Improved Turle Knot

(continued on next page)

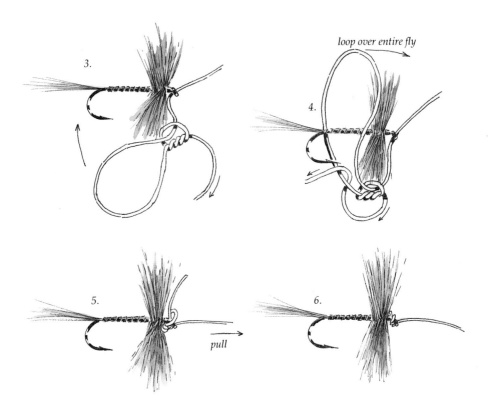

Finishing the Improved Turle Knot

GETTING READY FOR THE WATER
• •

Most fly-rod manufacturers provide a hard tube to protect the rod. If your rod tube comes with a screw-off cap, pocket the cap when you remove it so it doesn't get lost.

Inside most metal rod tubes, a cloth bag prevents the rod from banging around. When you remove the rod, stuff the bag back into the tube so you don't lose it.

Assemble the rod by sliding the sections together so the metal line guides line up. If the connections feel sandy, rinse both ends with plenty of water.

Be sure the connections are tight enough so the rod won't fly apart when you cast, but not so tight that you have difficulty pulling them apart.

THE REEL

On the bottom of your fly reel is a wing-shaped base, or "foot," that fits into the groove at the bottom of your fly rod, called the "reel seat."

If you are right-handed, you probably ought to have a reel you crank with your left hand (unless you are used to fishing with a standard level-wind bait-casting reel).

Slide the reel foot onto the reel seat and tighten it in place with the threaded rings that slide over the reel foot. With the rod tip pointing away from you, the reel handle should be to your left.

THREADING AND STRAIGHTENING THE LINE

If you are fishing with another angler, ask your companion to hold the grip of your rod as you thread the line through the metal guides. If you are alone, put your hat on the ground and rest the bottom of the rod on it to keep dirt from getting into the reel.

Pull the entire leader and about twelve feet of fly line off the reel. Double the fly line over on itself about a foot below the leader knot. Thread the doubled fly line up through the metal guides starting with the widest guide at the bottom. Please do not pass the fly line through that little metal loop near the cork handle; that is a hook keeper, a place to temporarily hold your fly when you're not fishing.

When the fly line is threaded through the top guide, pull the leader through, too, or wave the rod tip back and forth and the leader will fly out on its own.

DON'T LOSE YOUR TOP

To prevent losing the screw top from your rod tube, connect it to the tube:

Near the top of the rod tube, attach a plastic tie used to bundle electrical wires. The ties are available at hardware stores and automobile-parts suppliers. Drill a tiny hole in the center of the cap, and thread a piece of heavy monofilament line through it. Tie a large knot on the line on the inside of the cap to prevent it from pulling out. Tie the other end of the line to the plastic tie around the rod tube, and the cap won't get lost.

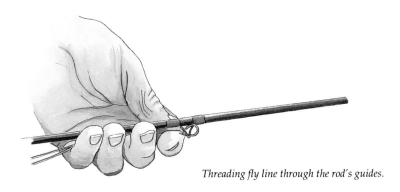

Threading fly line through the rod's guides.

If the leader has been wound on the reel for awhile, it may have become coiled or kinky. Run it through tightly squeezed fingers as you stretch it; the friction you create will warm and soften the leader so it straightens.

As you run your fingers down the leader, feel for rough spots that could weaken it. Before you start fishing, replace the rough section or the entire leader.

Next, straighten the fly line: If you are fishing with a buddy, ask your companion to pull thirty or forty feet of line straight out from the tip and pull on it until it stretches slightly. If you are fishing alone, pull out the same length of fly line and double it around a stout tree to stretch it slightly. If the weather is very cold, stretching the line too much may crack its surface, so beware.

Before you tie on a fly and start fishing, put on a pair of glasses to protect your eyes.

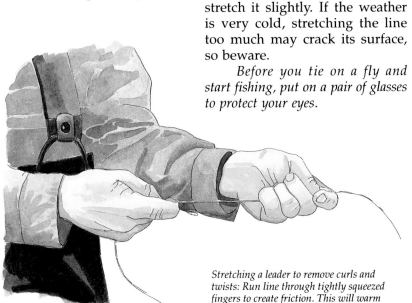

Stretching a leader to remove curls and twists: Run line through tightly squeezed fingers to create friction. This will warm and soften the leader so it straightens.

DISASSEMBLING YOUR GEAR

After the last cast of the day, squeeze your line in a sheet of paper towel as you reel it in. The towel will dry it and remove any weeds or dirt that the line may have accumulated. As you reel in the line through the paper towel, guide it onto the spool so it winds on uniformly, and leave about eight inches of leader sticking out of the reel so the end is easy to find the next time you go fishing.

Clip off the fly and squeeze it in the paper towel, too, before returning it to your fly box.

To take apart your fly rod, grasp each section near the joint, or ferrule, and pull the sections straight apart. Please do not hold onto the metal line guides; they bend easily. If you need more leverage, hold the rod behind your knees and use your legs to help push your hands and the rod sections apart. If you are fishing with a companion and the rod sections are stuck, each of you should hold both sections, as shown in the illustration, and pull in opposite directions.

Before you return the rod to its tube, wipe it dry and be certain the rod bag is dry, too. If you have been fishing in salt water, rinse the rod in fresh water as soon as you can.

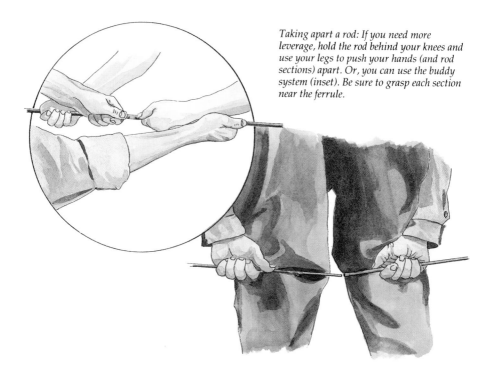

Taking apart a rod: If you need more leverage, hold the rod behind your knees and use your legs to push your hands (and rod sections) apart. Or, you can use the buddy system (inset). Be sure to grasp each section near the ferrule.

CARING FOR YOUR REEL AND FLY LINE

Please do not rinse a salt-water reel with a high-pressure hose; this may force salt and sand particles deeper into the reel. Instead, remove the line spool and soak both the spool and the rest of the reel in two or three freshwater baths, rinse them gently under a faucet, and dry them thoroughly before storing in a cool, dark, and well-ventilated place.

Washing your freshwater reels occasionally is a good idea. Follow the reel manufacturer's advice for lubricating the machinery with a high-quality reel grease, available at most fishing-tackle stores.

Most fly lines require only gentle soap and plenty of water to keep them clean and performing well, but you also may use a special line-cleaning substance that not only cleans the line, but makes it slicker so it casts easier. Several brands of line cleaner are available at fly shops.

Please do not let your fly line come in contact with sunscreen, insect repellent, bright sunlight streaming through your windshield, or the bottom of your feet, all of which can ruin it.

IN A NUTSHELL

1. Practice tying the Duncan Loop and Surgeon's Knot to handle most freshwater fly-fishing situations.

2. Keep your gear clean and store it in a cool, dark, well-ventilated place to maintain its peak performance on the water.

3. Be kind to your fly line and it will reward you with easy casting.

3

CASTING A FLY LINE

> **❝**Bill Koll, a three-time NCAA wrestling
> champ, was one of the greatest ever to walk
> onto a mat. I'll always remember something
> he once told me: The most primary and basic
> moves, refined and done to perfection, become
> the most advanced moves.**❞**
>
> **—JOE HUMPHREYS**
> Joe Humphreys's Trout Tactics, Updated and Expanded.

Most of the fish you catch with a fly rod will be within thirty feet of you, so don't worry about having to cast for distance. It is far more important to get close to fish and to control your line and leader so your fly behaves like living prey.

As you learn to cast, relax. Strength is not important. Casting a fly line requires timing and a little rhythm.

Practice whenever you can find the time, and soon you will *feel* each good cast. It is rhythmic and relaxing. Effortless.

When you botch a cast, don't worry; *everyone* does. Make one more good cast, enjoy how it feels, and remember the feeling so you can repeat it comfortably, effortlessly.

And don't worry about distance.

THE STROKE
· · · · · · · · · · · · · · ·

To propel a fly line, your forearm and hand move backward and forward. The movement looks like a V with your elbow at the bottom of it. That's the basic casting stroke. It's exactly like the motion you'd use to throw a chunk of potato off the tines of a dinner fork. Imagine doing that.

Unlike the stroke in other sports, the fly-casting motion has no follow-through. *The basic stroke requires only two short bursts of speed, one accelerating straight backward with a quick STOP and one accelerating straight forward with a quick STOP.*

If you can go outdoors now, try throwing a chunk of raw potato off a dinner fork. It may sound weird, but give it a shot.

Keep your wrist rigid and your elbow relaxed by your side. First, throw a potato chunk behind you, up and over your shoulder. Still relaxed but with your wrist rigid, throw another piece of potato forward, up and away from you.

If you try the potato exercise, you will see that the chunk takes off when you snap and STOP the stroke. The potato flies where the tip of the fork is pointing at the snap-STOP. That's exactly how the fly-casting stroke works: The line flies where the rod tip is pointing when you snap-STOP the stroke.

Start practicing the casting stroke without holding the fly rod.

Imagine that you're gripping a house-painting brush with the bristles pointing upward. Your elbow is at your side, just above your waist.

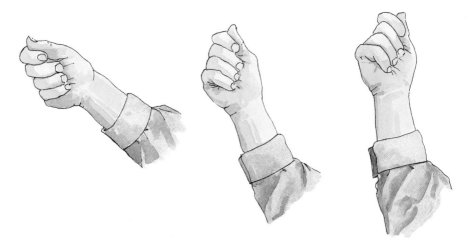

Practicing your casting stroke with a rod. A good cast is rhythmic and relaxing.

Previous page: "Foggy Day"—Agulukpak River, Alaska.

Now lift your thumb so the top of the thumb points toward the sky. Imagine that your thumb is pressing against the brush.

Relax your shoulder and upper arm. Strength is not important.

Try to keep your wrist rigid so your forearm does all the work.

With your elbow relaxed near your waist, snap your forearm backward toward your shoulder and STOP. That's the backcast.

With another short burst of speed, snap your forearm forward so your hand travels about ten inches and STOP. That's the forward cast.

To practice the stroke, relax and remember the rhythm: Back-snap-STOP. Forward-snap-STOP. Back-snap-STOP. Forward-snap-STOP.

Here's another exercise to help you learn the stroke and the importance of the STOP.

Pretend that the paint brush you're holding is soaked with paint. Spatter an imaginary wall behind you with a stroke up and over your shoulder. Now spatter an imaginary wall in front of you at eye level.

Repeat the motion, but *don't get any paint on the ceiling*. Keep your wrist rigid. Now snap the brush straight back and STOP, and then straight forward and STOP. If you move it in an arc, as though you're tracing a rainbow, you'll get paint on the ceiling.

Try the spattering exercise with water: Dip the tip of your forefinger into a glass of water. With your elbow relaxed near your waist, and your wrist rigid, snap your forearm backward and STOP. See how far to the rear you can flick water drops. Wet your forefinger again and with another short burst of speed, snap your forearm forward and STOP. Watch how far the water drops fly when you STOP.

Relax and remember the rhythm: Back-snap-STOP. Forward-snap-STOP. Back-snap-STOP. Forward-snap-STOP.

WATCH YOUR ROD TIP

As you practice casting, watch the top of the rod. When you begin the stroke, notice how it bends: It is acting like a spring, "loading" itself to throw the line. That part of the stroke is smooth. As your forearm accelerates toward the snap-STOP, the rod bends deeper, and the snap-STOP propels the line to wherever the rod tip is pointing.

Watch the "loop" that forms in the line and try to shape it so it looks like a candy cane coming off the tip of the rod. If the loop is too open, your arm is probably moving in an arc, instead of straight backward and straight forward.

THE FOUR-PART CAST
• •

When you understand the stroke, it's time to learn the four-part cast. It will become easy for you, so relax.

The four elements of the cast are:

1. Pickup

2. Back-snap-STOP

3. Forward-snap-STOP

4. Present the line to the water

You can practice the four-part cast on a lawn or on still water, as long as you have about thirty feet of space behind you and about the same amount of space in front of you. Also, you need your fly rod and reel, spooled with backing and a fly line. Attach the thick end of a seven-foot leader to the end of the fly line.

Remember how to string the rod? Pull several feet of line off the reel, and near the tip of the line, fold it over on itself and thread it through the wire loops, called guides. Don't thread the line through that tiny piece of wire next to the cork grip, however: That's a hook keeper. When you have passed the folded line through the tip-top guide, pull the leader through.

Now tie a small, brightly colored fly to the leader tippet. With a pair of wire cutters, clip off the hook point to create a practice fly. Tying a wisp of bright yarn at the end of your leader also works.

If you're practicing alone, put the rod down and pull out about thirty feet of line. Stretch it out in front of you. (Eventually, you'll get the line out by pulling it off the reel and wiggling the rod tip.)

Walk back to the rod, and pick it up by the cork handle, *but keep the rod tip low*, only an inch off the grass or the water. *You must keep slack out of the line when making a cast.* Starting with the rod tip low is important.

With your throwing hand, grip the rod handle with your fingers on the bottom and your thumbnail facing up. Hold it firmly, but not so tight that your fingers start to cramp.

With your other hand, reach out about two feet above the reel and grab the line. Hold it with that hand, your line hand, next to your belt buckle. *Keep the rod tip low.*

Stand squarely facing the practice area and, for better balance, place the foot below your rod hand slightly behind the other foot.

Relax.

To start the four-part cast, the end of the line must be moving; that's the job of the pickup. Relax your elbow near your waist and keep your wrist rigid as you lift the rod smoothly. If you feel more

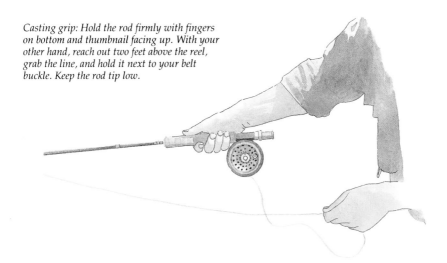

Casting grip: Hold the rod firmly with fingers on bottom and thumbnail facing up. With your other hand, reach out two feet above the reel, grab the line, and hold it next to your belt buckle. Keep the rod tip low.

comfortable with your elbow away from your body, that's all right as long as most of the motion for the cast is coming from your forearm, not your wrist.

Smoothly lift the rod closer to the point where you normally start the back-snap-STOP, and get ready for that short burst of speed.

Accelerate your forearm into the back-snap-STOP. The line will fly over your shoulder and behind you. Turn your head to watch it.

As the fly line starts to straighten out behind you, accelerate your forearm into the forward-snap-STOP. The line will fly over you, folded over in the shape of a candy cane. (In fly-fishing jargon, that's a "loop.")

The pick-up: Accelerate your forearm into the back-snap-STOP. Most of the motion for the cast should come from your forearm, not your wrist.

The back cast: Go high and hard, then wait.
Let the rod "load up."

The moment the line straightens out, gently lower the rod tip to the water and present the line. The front of the line, the leader, and the practice fly should flutter down gently.

Always start the cast with the rod tip next to the water to keep slack out of the line. Keep your wrist rigid, and remember the rhythm. As you practice, whisper the elements of the cast to yourself: *pickup with a back-snap-STOP. Forward-snap-STOP. Present the line.*

One more thing to remember: Relax. The less you exert yourself, the smoother the cast will be.

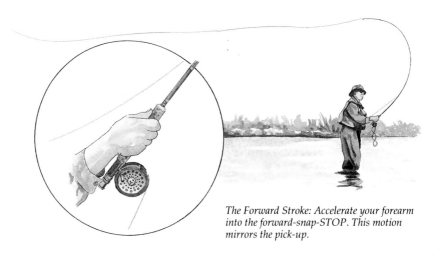

The Forward Stroke: Accelerate your forearm
into the forward-snap-STOP. This motion
mirrors the pick-up.

After *the line straightens out, lower your rod tip to the water and present the line.*

SOLUTIONS

If the fly line is falling in a heap in front of you or behind you, you may be swishing the rod back and forth with a loose wrist. Try to keep your wrist more rigid. Some beginning casters like to use athletic tape on the casting wrist. Others stick the bottom of the rod—the butt—into a sleeve cuff to keep the wrist rigid. As casting becomes more comfortable, you may develop a slight wrist snap, but for now keep your wrist rigid and let your forearm do the work.

To remember where to STOP the stroke, some casters like to imagine they're standing next to a giant clock, facing nine o'clock, with twelve o'clock directly overhead. The forearm accelerates into the backcast and it stops when the rod tip points to one o'clock. The forward cast stops when the thumb points at ten o'clock. Eventually, your stroke will shorten for very short casts and lengthen to achieve more distance. For now, concentrate on casting about thirty feet of line accurately.

When you hear the rod whooshing through a back-snap-STOP or a forward-snap-STOP, you may be applying too much power to the cast. Relax and remember: *The stroke requires only two short bursts of speed, one accelerating straight backward with a quick STOP and one accelerating straight forward with a quick STOP.*

When the line makes a cracking noise, like a whip, it probably means that you're starting the forward-snap-STOP a little too quickly. Just pause a bit. When you complete the back-snap-STOP, whisper "Yellowstone" and *then* start the forward-snap-STOP.

If the line snags on the grass behind you, one of these solutions may help: Start the forward-snap-STOP sooner, so the line doesn't have time to fall to the ground. Imagine that you're going to throw the line *up* over your shoulder rather than behind you. Or, imagine that you're standing next to the giant clock, facing nine o'clock. STOP the backcast with the rod tip pointing at twelve o'clock.

The best way to solve most early casting problems is to relax and practice the basic stroke: Back-snap-STOP. Forward-snap STOP.

TWO-POINT CONTROL

Until now, your line hand has been holding the fly line next to your belt buckle. If you were fishing with your line hand in that position, you'd have trouble animating a fly that's supposed to look like a swimming creature. You'd have even more trouble retrieving line if a fish struck at your fly.

Two-point control of your fly line solves these problems. It's easy:

Continue to cast as you have been—with your line hand holding the fly line next to your belt buckle. When you complete the four-part cast, lowering the rod tip makes the fly line, leader, and fly flutter to the surface. At that moment, switch the line from your line hand to your rod hand and tuck the fly line under your middle finger, next to the cork handle.

With the fly line anchored between your finger and the cork, your line hand is free to retrieve line. And if a fish bites, all you have to do is raise the rod tip quickly to set the hook into the fish's jaw.

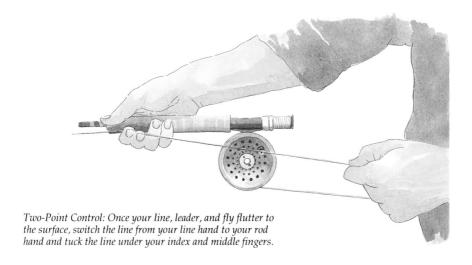

Two-Point Control: Once your line, leader, and fly flutter to the surface, switch the line from your line hand to your rod hand and tuck the line under your index and middle fingers.

As soon as you start fly fishing, you're bound to believe that professional fly tiers spend their free time planting trees trained to reach out and grab flies. Getting snagged is part of the sport; it happens to everyone, not just beginners.

If you do get snagged on a forward cast, don't try to throw your fly line through the branches; it will make things worse. Instead, try this technique explained by Joe Humphreys:

Point your rod tip at the snagged fly and retrieve fly line with your hand until the line tightens against the snag. When the line tightens, release it from your line hand so it springs back toward the snag. Often this will free the fly, but you may have to repeat the maneuver a couple of times.

FALSE CASTING

Flies that float—dry flies—sometimes get soaked and start to sink. To dry a waterlogged fly, use a false cast. Here's how it works:

Pull about fifteen feet of fly line from the rod tip, and get ready to start the four-part cast.

With the rod tip low, nearly touching the grass or water in front of you, start the cast: pickup and back-snap-STOP.

Now forward-snap-STOP.

Instead of lowering the rod tip, however, start another back-snap-STOP, then a forward-snap-STOP.

Straight backward and straight forward, backward and forward, move the rod with a quick STOP at the end of each movement to keep the fly line in the air. If you imagine that you are standing next to the giant clock, facing nine o'clock, watch your casting hand and STOP the back-snap-STOP when the rod tip points at one o'clock. Stop the forward-snap-STOP when the rod tip points at eleven o'clock. The stroke is brief.

The STOP throws the fly line. As the line straightens, it shakes water off the fly. After three or four sets of backward and forward strokes, STOP the rod in front of you and lower the tip to present the line. When the dry fly flutters to the water's surface, it should float.

False casting also is an effective way of practicing the fly-casting stroke. Watch the loop as the line comes off the rod tip and try to make it look like a candy cane.

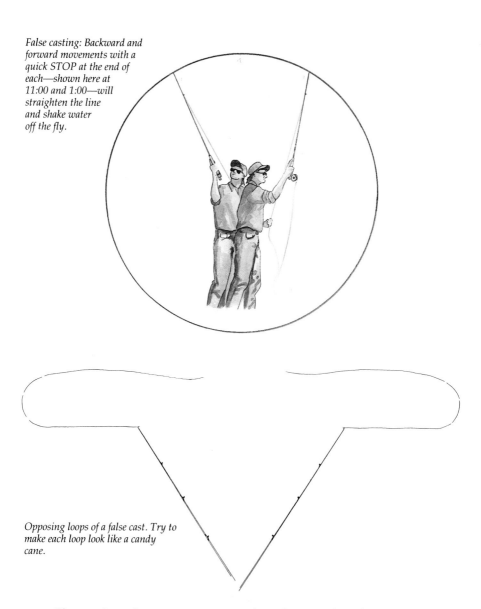

False casting: Backward and forward movements with a quick STOP at the end of each—shown here at 11:00 and 1:00—will straighten the line and shake water off the fly.

Opposing loops of a false cast. Try to make each loop look like a candy cane.

If your loop is too open, remember the paintbrush exercise: The object is to spatter paint on the imaginary wall behind you and the imaginary wall in front of you *without* getting paint on the ceiling. If you move your hand in an arc, as though you're tracing a rainbow, you'll spatter the ceiling.

Relax, and remember: The stroke requires only two short bursts of speed, one accelerating straight backward with a quick STOP and one accelerating straight forward with a quick STOP.

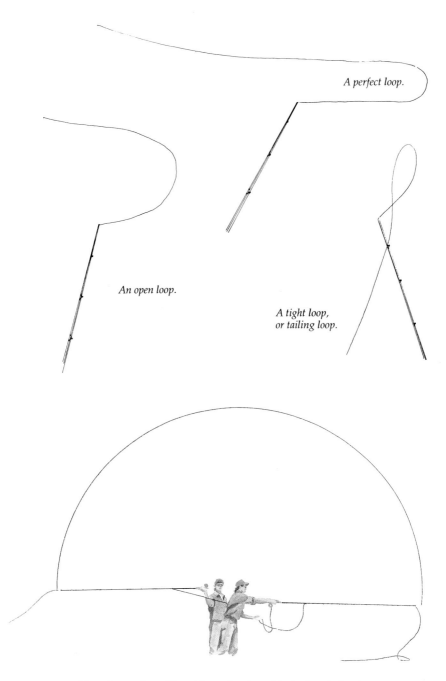

A perfect loop.

An open loop.

A tight loop,
or tailing loop.

Throwing a collapsed loop: The arc here is too big; in the paintbrush
exercise, this would spatter paint on the ceiling.

SHOOTING LINE

If you started the false-casting exercise with fifteen feet of fly line out of the rod tip, you finished with the same amount of line out there. Imagine that you're fishing, and you spot a fish feeding farther away. To get your fly to the fish you must "shoot" some line.

It's easy.

You already have fifteen feet of line stretched out in front of you, and as you hold the rod its tip is low, nearly touching the grass or the water.

With your free hand, or line hand, pull nine or ten feet of line off the reel—three long yanks. Let the line fall at your feet, but be careful not to step on it.

Now, with your line hand, reach out about two feet above the reel and grab the line and hold it next to your belt buckle. *Keep the rod tip low*, only an inch off the grass or the water.

Imagine what you're going to do:

Pick up with a back-snap-STOP. Forward-snap-STOP.

At that moment, open your line hand and the fly line at your feet will shoot through the rod guides and out the tip.

When the fly line straightens out in the air in front of you, present the line: Lower the rod tip so the fly line, leader, and fly gently flutter down.

Use two-point control by bringing your line hand to your rod hand, and tuck the fly line beneath your middle finger, against the cork handle.

Now try it. Start by "stripping" in some fly line: With your line hand, pull the fly line, about a foot at a time, back through the line guides, toward the reel. When you're fishing, you strip line to animate flies resembling baitfish, leeches, and other swimming creatures. Keep the rod tip nearly touching the grass or the water in front of you. With the fly line between the middle finger of your rod hand and the cork, use your line hand to pull about ten feet of fly line back toward you— about a foot at a time. Let the stripped line fall at your feet.

To start the cast, keep the rod tip low and bring your line hand to your rod hand. Remove the fly line from beneath your middle finger and hold it in your line hand next to your belt buckle.

Start with a pickup and a back-snap-STOP. Forward-snap-STOP and release the fly line. It will fly out the tip. When the fly line straightens in the air, lower the rod tip and tuck the fly line beneath the middle finger of your rod hand for two-point control.

THE ROLL CAST
• • • • • • • • • • • • • • • • • • •

Until now, you've started each practice session by walking the fly line out of the rod tip. That might be impractical when you go fishing.

Try this: With about nine or ten feet of fly line (a little longer than the rod) hanging out of the rod tip, pull another ten feet of line off the reel and let it fall at your feet.

Holding the rod with the tip near the water, wave it from right to left in wide sweeps until all of the line at your feet snakes its way through the rod tip. That's much easier than walking the fly line out, isn't it? Now all you have to do is straighten the line out in front of you.

Enter the roll cast. It is easy to learn, but you must practice on water. Here's how it works:

With your line hand, reach out and grasp the fly line above the cork grip and hold it near your belt buckle.

Tilt your rod hand so your thumb tip points up and away from your body. Now slowly move the rod so the tip points up and over your shoulder. If you imagine that you're standing next to a clock, facing nine o'clock, the rod tip is pointing at one o'clock, behind you.

The fly line hanging off the rod tip will drape itself behind you.

Pause and let the line on the water become still.

Loading the rod for a roll cast. Move the rod so the tip points up and over your shoulder. If you're facing 9:00, the rod tip will point to 1:00 behind you, with the line draping itself behind you. Remember to hesitate.

Now accelerate the rod into a forward-snap-STOP. Remember, the fly line will go in the direction the rod tip is pointing when it stops.

Watch the line roll on the water's surface and straighten out in front of you. Lower the rod tip to the water's surface and tuck the fly line beneath the middle finger of your rod hand so you have two-point control.

Roll cast forward stroke: Accelerate the rod into a forward-snap-STOP—and don't go too low.

It's that easy.

The roll cast is especially useful when there is not enough room behind you for a standard four-part cast. To extend the distance of your fly, do a series of roll casts, pulling more line off the reel for each cast until you achieve the distance you want.

PRACTICE
• • • • • • • • • • •

Now that you have mastered the four-part cast and the roll cast, try throwing each of them to the side away from your body and to the other side, across your chest. Mastering the casts to your side will help you deal with wind and with trees hanging low over the water.

With a little practice, fly casting will feel comfortable and rhythmic. Effortless.

When you start to enjoy the rhythm of casting, shoot for accuracy; cast to buckets on the lawn or to rings on the water. To catch fish, accuracy is much more important than distance.

Casting does not require strength, only timing, as your arm accelerates to a STOP. If your muscles feel cramped or your cast seems to fall apart while practicing, it's time to take a break, grab a dinner fork, and pitch a potato.

Complete the roll cast by rolling the line out on the water's surface. To present the line, lower the rod tip to the water's surface and move your hands into a two-point control position.

Kneeling on a bonefish flat, sitting in a canoe: you're going to find yourself casting from many different positions as you explore the world of fly fishing. It's important to simulate real fishing conditions as you practice casting.

A folding chair is a great practice aid. Place it at the edge of the water or on the lawn, sit down, and relax. The chair will force you to aim the rod tip higher when you STOP the cast behind you. That will make you a more effective fisher when you're casting from a float tube or a canoe, and it will keep your fly from snagging on grass behind you.

IN A NUTSHELL

1. Relax, and remember: The basic casting stroke requires only two short bursts of speed, one accelerating straight backward with a quick STOP and one accelerating straight forward with a quick STOP. As you accelerate your forearm, watch the top of the rod to be certain that it is bending, or "loading" itself to throw the fly line. When you STOP the rod, the line will fly in the direction the rod tip is pointing.

2. To start the four-part cast and to complete it, keep the rod tip low, next to the water. This helps to keep slack out of the line.

3. In the beginning, it helps to keep your wrist rigid, and your upper arm and elbow relaxed as you let your forearm do the work.

4. Don't worry about distance. Timing and accuracy are more important for catching fish.

4

UNDERSTANDING AND SIMULATING FISH FOODS

"The Green Drake nearly spoiled me rotten.
During its hectic presence I became careless
again about my casting, about my position,
about whether or not the trout took me for a
cow or thought they were making huge plump
herons this year—and mostly it did not
matter. If a trout had the sweet tooth for a
drake, if it seemed so determined to risk its
skin to get one, I could understand: I feel that
way about duck-liver pâté, country style.**"**

—NICK LYONS
Spring Creek

Fish lead dual lives: They are predators and prey.

As predators, fish are opportunists. Whenever the opportunity
arises, they will eat anything that appears to be edible, including other
fish, insects, and even small birds and mammals that blunder into the
water. Predatory fish are efficient: They attack when their prey appears

Extended-body flies.

to be fleeing, crippled, or so abundant that it will be easy to get without expending much energy.

From the time a fish is born, however, it is prey to other creatures, including larger fish, some aquatic insects, and fish-eating birds and mammals. A fish quickly learns to flee from anything that appears to be a threat.

To catch fish, you must determine what they are eating. Then you can simulate the natural prey with an artificial fly that appears to be real food and behaves as though it is alive.

Before you start fishing, watch the water as a predator. Be still and look for places where fish can get plenty of food to eat and oxygen to breathe with little effort. Watch the surface of the water for a disturbance such as a ring or a bulge that indicates a fish is feeding.

On the water's surface, look for living creatures that fish may eat. Through your polarized sunglasses, peer beneath the surface to see if any small fish are swimming there. Lift rocks off the bottom to see what kinds of prey live on the bottom.

Observe the size, shape, and color of the natural prey so you can select the artificial fly that matches what the fish are eating. Then watch how the prey behaves so you can make your fly appear to be alive.

In the back of this book, you will find lists of recommended artificial flies to carry. When you are fishing, the challenge is to select the one that fish are most likely to take as real food.

THE INSECTS FISH EAT

Freshwater fish eat aquatic insects, bugs born on the bottom of streams and ponds. Aquatic insects spend most of their lives beneath the surface of the water, a violent world where they are easy prey for fish.

Beneath the water, the bodies of aquatic insects change again and again as they grow to become adults; as they drift along with currents or swim to find food, the immature insects are targets for attack.

Then they emerge from the water and shuck their skin to become airborne adults. Some insects struggle to shed their old bodies, and as they hang in the top layer of water, the film, the "emergers" again are easy prey for fish.

Some insects float along as they dry their wings before flying away; fish wait just beneath the surface and snatch the adult insects from the film. Other insects pop to the surface and immediately fly away, and as they flee, fish leap out of the water to catch the bugs.

Scientists and anglers have written many books about the insects that freshwater fish eat. As a fly fisher, you can devote a lifetime to learning about these fascinating bugs, or you can simply simulate what you see in the water to catch fish. Here are some of the insects you will find and some ideas about how to make them look alive.

MAYFLIES

An important food for trout, bass, and panfish, mayflies are born on the bottoms of streams as well as still waters. In their various stages of development, they provide a constant source of food for trout and other gamefish.

THE NYMPH After hatching from its egg, a mayfly spends

Mayfly

about a year beneath the water as a nymph. As it grows, the nymph continually molts, shedding its armor-plated skin for the next size up. The nymphs of some mayfly species are so minuscule that several can fit on one of your fingernails. Others are as long as the distance from one of your knuckles to the next. Most mayfly nymphs are camouflaged, resembling the color of their environment, usually dull brown, olive, or copper. Immediately after molting, many mayfly nymphs look milky. Some are excellent swimmers, but others are not and they get caught up in the current.

To learn what kind of mayfly nymphs are in the water, look at rocks from the bottom or use a fly fisher's fine-mesh net to catch nymphs living in the gravel.

To select an artificial fly that simulates the most prevalent nymphs you find, first match the size and shape of the real nymphs. Then select a similar color.

In flowing water, the current catches nymphs and washes them down to waiting fish. To simulate a drifting nymph, cast your artificial fly so it hits the water above a spot where you suspect a fish to be hiding. Cast it far enough above the spot so it has time to sink to the fish's level. If the current is quick, you may have to use a weighted fly or a sinking-tip fly line, or add weight to your leader to help your fly sink. *When fish are feeding on the bottom, you must adjust the weight on your leader frequently to keep your fly near the fish.*

As you gain more experience, you will discover many ways to fish an artificial nymph. In the beginning, however, position yourself up-current from the fish's hiding spot and cast the nymph across and slightly down the current.

Sometimes, as the line swings in the water to straighten itself in the current, it makes the nymph look as though it is swimming to the surface. If a fish senses that the nymph is going to get away, the preda-

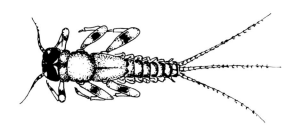

Nymph

tor may attack. If you can see a fish feeding beneath the surface, you can animate your fly to stimulate the same response: Cast your nymph up-current of the fish and allow it to drift right to the fish. Then, just as your fly is about to reach the fish, lift your rod and fly line to make the fly rise and appear as though it is going to escape.

Remember: If something looks edible and appears to be fleeing, a predator is likely to attack it.

EMERGERS   After a year beneath the water, mayfly nymphs rise to the surface, where they shed their nymphal armor to fly away and live a brief life as an adult.

When many members of the same species emerge at once, fly fishers call it a "hatch." The fish sense that the hatch offers an opportunity to eat plenty of food, and their predatory instinct seizes that opportunity. Because they cannot afford to expend too much effort eating, they target the most abundant food source, often rejecting larger food items. This behavior is called "selective feeding."

During a hatch, the first stage of a mayfly's adulthood is as an emerger, climbing out of the nymph's body. Eating nymphs about to emerge, fish often reveal their presence by "bulging" the water just beneath the surface. Try to scoop up some nymphs from beneath the surface so you can match their size, shape, and color with an artificial fly. Then grease your leader with floatant so it suspends your fly just beneath the surface where the fish are feeding.

As the emerger struggles out of its shell, it also must puncture through the water's surface film, which is like an elastic skin. Some emergers spend a long time in the film, and others are too weak to break away completely. The film traps and drowns them, making them easy prey for fish. Artificial emergers, flush in the surface film, often fool feeding fish.

DUNS AND SPINNERS   When a mayfly emerges from the water, it unfurls its smoky-gray wings and floats atop the water until they dry. Called a dun, it looks like a miniature sailboat as it floats atop the water. To simulate this stage of the mayfly, use a dry fly with upright wings, matching the size, shape, and color of the natural fly, and allow it to float naturally.

The unnatural movement of a dry fly, called "drag," repels fish.

In moving water, the current's pressure against the fly line or the leader causes drag. It makes the fly float slower or faster than live insects floating on the water. You will know drag has set in when the fly makes a V-shaped wake on the surface and when it floats at a different speed than flecks of foam or leaves on the water. Changing your position will help eliminate drag, and so will mending, discussed in the

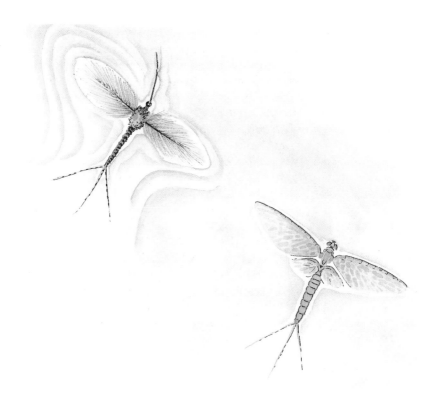

*Watching the movement of an artificial and natural spinner on the water will help you understand how drag can make a fly look un*natural.

chapter on tactics for making your fly look alive.

To simulate a live mayfly dun, you must eliminate drag. Allowing the fly to float naturally with the current is called a "dead drift."

As soon as the dun's wings are dry, the insect leaves the water and flies to the trees, where its body changes again. Within hours, the dun's shell splits open and a "spinner" emerges. On glassy wings, spinners fly about to mate, then the females hover above the water and dip to its surface, depositing their eggs. Spent of eggs and strength, they fall and die, wings askew, bodies flush in the surface film.

Like the hatch, the fall of many spinners triggers fish to begin another feeding binge. To catch fish, a spinner imitation must float without drag.

CADDISFLIES
. . . .

Freshwater fish also eat caddisflies, also called sedge flies, which look like moths when they become adults.

LARVAE AND PUPAE Hatching from its egg, a caddis becomes a wormlike larva. Some surround themselves with cases made of sand grains while others use sticks or bits of vegetation, bound together with silk that they excrete from their mouths. The larvae of other caddis species live free of a case. Fly tiers have devised many artificial flies to simulate cased and free-living larvae. On flowing water, cast a larva imitation up-current of fish and allow it to dead drift near the bottom, simulating a live larva caught in the flow.

Six months to a year after it is born, a caddis larva matures to become a pupa. As it matures, an adult body forms inside the pupa. Then the adult cuts its way out of its pupal skin, or chamber. Some species climb out of the water as they emerge, and others swim to shore.

ADULTS The most exciting fishing, however, occurs when caddisflies emerge on the surface. The emerging adult generates gasses that float it to the surface. As it rises, its pupal shell expands and bursts, and the adult pops out of the water. Some species emerge with such speed that fish leap out of the water after them.

Other species have to pause for a moment before taking off. As they test their wings, buzzing about the surface, the new adults are attractive prey for fish beneath them.

Whenever you see trout splashing on the surface, the fish probably are feeding on emerging caddisflies. Fly tiers have developed many artificial flies to simulate emerging caddisflies, and several wet flies also work well.

Animate artificial caddisflies to appear as though they are rising to the surface, about to escape. When you see a fish splashing at emergers, cast your fly up-current, allow it to dead drift to the

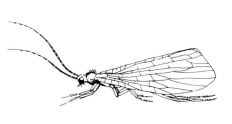

Caddisfly

fish, and just before it arrives, lift your rod and fly line to raise the fly.

STONEFLIES
• • • • • • • • • • • • • •

Find a clean, bubbly stream and you probably will find stoneflies, a staple in the diet of trout in waters bristling with oxygen.

Fish gobble up adult stoneflies, also called salmon flies, when the insects emerge from the water. Trout probably eat more nymphs than

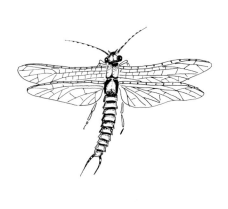

Stonefly

adults, however, because the immature insects are more abundant most of the time. The nymphs range in size from less than a half-inch long to the giant stoneflies of the American West, which are as long as three inches. They have two tails.

Stonefly nymphs emerge from the water throughout the year, usually crawling onto an exposed boulder or the shore. The adult stonefly breaks out of the nymph's armor, leaving its former shell behind. On many western rivers, stonefly husks cover entire boulders and bridge abutments where the nymphs crawled out.

On some western streams, stoneflies are the trout's principal food source. When the adults are not hatching, you will need a strong leader to fish large, weighted imitation nymphs. To catch fish, animate the fly so it looks like a big bug swimming beneath the water: Cast it across the current, and as the flow sweeps it down, twitch the fly with your line hand, pulling in small lengths of fly line.

The wings of artificial stonefly adults sweep back over buoyant bodies—like the real insect.

In the East, where anglers sometimes mistake small stoneflies for caddisflies, artificial caddisflies often will fool fish feeding on little stoneflies.

On some western streams, so many real stoneflies emerge at once that your artificial fly can get lost in the crowd. When you find yourself in such a massive hatch, find a fish that is feeding steadily on the surface and cast your fly to make it alight just up-current from the fish, and let it float to the trout without any unnatural movement, or drag.

If you are convinced that your fly is the same size, shape, and color as those of real stoneflies on the water but the fish continue to refuse it, try this: Just before the fly floats over the fish, twitch it slightly. Sometimes, animating a floating fly triggers a predatory fish to attack.

TWO-WINGED FLIES

Mosquitoes and midges, those bothersome bugs you can barely see, belong to a huge group of insects that fish eat. Their scientific name is Diptera: *di* means "two," and *ptera* means "wings." Horseflies and deerflies also belong to this group, with more than 8,000 members in North America.

On slow streams and many ponds, two-winged flies are so numerous that fish depend on the insects as a principal food source.

Minuscule midges are especially important. On many waters, they emerge throughout the year. Fish eat the midge's wormlike larva, the first stage of the insect's life, as well as the pupa, which often suspends itself in the water's surface film just before the adult breaks out of the pupa's skin to fly away. Generally, you should not animate flies simulating midge larvae and pupae; in nature, they simply drift with the current. Cast the fly so it lands on the water above the fish, with plenty of time to sink. If you can see the fish, watch for its head to turn slightly or look for its white mouth to open quickly to take your fly. Then lift your rod to set the hook.

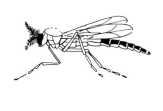

Midge

The midge's much larger relative, the crane-fly larva, does wiggle as it moves in the flow, so you should animate imitation crane-fly "worms" by slightly twitching the fly line after the fly sinks.

Flies imitating adult midges and crane-flies are fuzzy to make them appear as though they are hovering on the water's surface. On most occasions, you should allow them to float in the current without drag. When fish are not responding, however, you may be able to trigger a strike by "skating" the fly: Cast the fly across the current, then hold your rod tip high to keep line off the water. A few inches at a time, pull the fly toward you so it appears to be skating weightlessly with the water's current.

DAMSELFLIES AND DRAGONFLIES

Among nature's oldest insects, damselflies and dragonflies are also among the largest. As adults, the needlelike insects are long, with jewel-bright bodies that hover above ponds and slow streams.

Large bass and trout prey on damselfly and dragonfly nymphs and adults. As nymphs with strong teeth, the insects get their "revenge" by eating small bass and trout, as well as other immature insects below the water's surface. The most effective imitations of the damselfly and dragonfly nymphs are made with soft materials that make them look alive as you pull them toward shore, simulating the real insect as it crawls out to emerge as an adult.

Fly tiers use deer hair, foam, and other buoyant materials to make the long and slender imitations of adult damselflies and dragonflies. On ponds, cast your fly to openings in beds of exposed weeds where you can see fish feeding on the surface. Approach as closely as possible to make an accurate cast to the spot where you saw a fish. When you hit the target, the fish may strike the moment the fly alights on the water. If a fish does not strike immediately, let the fly remain motionless for as long as you have patience. After the long wait, twitch the fly ever so slightly to provoke the fish beneath the surface.

On slow streams, cast the fly up-current from feeding bass and trout and let the imitation float down to them as though it were drowned.

Fish are savage when they strike damselflies and dragonflies.

LAND INSECTS

Ants, beetles, grasshoppers, and other insects living on land occasionally blunder into the water. Fish find something about them especially attractive—perhaps their flavor or size or their frantic movements on the surface. Even during a large emergence of aquatic insects, when fish key in on a single size and shape of bug, a terrestrial insect on the water can attract strikes.

Fly tiers usually use opaque materials to make imitation land insects; foam, balsa wood, and thick, lacquered feathers create solid profiles for the distinct shapes of ants, beetles, and other bugs. Soft feathers or fine strips of supple rubber simulate the thrashing legs of a grasshopper or cricket blown onto the water's surface.

On clear, slow-moving streams, watch for fish surface feeding tight against a grassy bank or just down-current from an overhanging

Damselfly

Grasshopper

tree or bush, particularly on windy days. It may be eating land insects blown onto the water. On the banks of a meadow stream, look for grasshoppers and beetles, then select an artificial fly that resembles the size and color of the real bugs. On a treelined stream, start with an artificial fly that looks like the ants, beetles, or worms in the leaves. Artificial crickets often work on wooded rivers as well as on meadow streams.

Approach a surface-feeding fish cautiously so you can get as close as possible. Cast your fly close to the bank, just up-current of the fish, and allow it to float tight to the bank. You can twitch the fly, but try to avoid drag, the current's pull on the line or leader, which causes your fly to throw a V-shaped wake on the water.

ATTRACTOR FLIES

Over generations, fly fishers have created artificial flies that look nothing like natural insects, but catch fish when nothing else will. Attractor flies such as the Royal Coachman and the Humpy may work precisely because they *do* look different.

To survive, fish must be curious about things that may be edible and nutritious; often, they strike twigs, seeds, and berries on the water's surface. When a big, buggy-looking thing comes floating along, it often will provoke an opportunistic predator to strike.

BAITFISH

Fish eat other fish, including their own offspring. Some fly fishers believe that trout prefer streamers that look like their own kind. Yellow-and-brown streamers, for example, seem to attract brown trout, while olive-and-pink flies trigger rainbow trout to strike.

Most fly tiers create streamer patterns to simulate minnows, but some famous flies, such as the Mickey Finn, a freshwater fly, and Lefty's Deceiver, a saltwater pattern, catch many fish even though, to the human eye, they resemble nothing in nature. That may be the key to their success.

Baitfish

Predators strike prey that appears to be escaping, crippled, or so abundant that it will be easy to get without expending much energy. When a predatory fish attacks a school of bait, the attacker looks for prey that appear to be different from the others. A baitfish with a torn cheek, exposing its blood-red gills, may appear to be an easy target. Saltwater bait fishers sometimes dip live baitfish in bright dye that makes their bait stand out from other potential prey in the eyes of a predator. The difference may account for the success of streamer patterns that look nothing like real baitfish.

More important than a streamer's colors are its movements. Predators look for baitfish on the edge of a school, crippled fish that will be easier to attack than strong prey. Such predators as chinook salmon swim through schools of herring, smashing the prey with their powerful tails to cripple the smaller fish. Disoriented, the injured herring swim in spirals, signaling the salmon that they are easy to take.

When you are simulating baitfish with a streamer, match the fly to the size of the natural bait, and animate it so it appears to be escaping, disoriented, or crippled. In fresh water, for example, make the fly swim near fish you can see, and then pull it away quickly. Or retrieve it erratically, so it looks injured.

On the edge of a strong current or in the surf, let the water animate the fly for you. A crippled minnow is at the mercy of moving water, and predators watch for bait being washed about.

Occasionally, fish will strike other fish to protect their offspring. Male bass, for instance, guard their nests and attack marauding sunfish. However, most fish, even large predators, flee from flies that appear to be on the attack. *Animate baitfish imitations so they appear to be escaping, never attacking.*

OTHER ANIMALS
• • • • • • • • • • • • • • • • • • • •

CRUSTACEANS Fly tiers have created many artificial flies to simulate shrimp, crabs, and other shelled creatures for saltwater fly fishing. Freshwater fly fishers use imitation crayfish and scuds, often called freshwater shrimp, to take a variety of fish including trout, bass, and panfish.

Most crustaceans camouflage themselves by changing color to match the environment. Look in weed beds for shrimp and similar creatures, and among rocks for crustaceans with harder shells, such as crayfish and, in salt water, small crabs. Match the size and color of the natural crustacean, and animate your fly so it looks alive, moving in short, quick spurts, as though it is trying to escape.

WORMS AND LEECHES Though they are entirely different animals, worms and leeches often share the same slow-moving water, and their similar undulating movements attract strikes. Many artificial flies made with soft furs and feathers look like real worms and leeches when you animate them to appear as though they are swimming along with the current or, in still water, as though they are escaping a predator.

Leech

SALAMANDERS, SNAKES, AND EELS Salamanders prey on fish eggs and water snakes eat fish. Bass, pike, and other freshwater fish may strike artificial salamanders and snakes as a form of self-defense or because the wiggly creatures represent large meals. Whatever the reason, imitation salamanders and snakes often provoke smashing strikes when you work them slowly over weed beds.

In salt water, eel imitations, also made with supple materials, attract bluefish and striped bass in northeastern estuaries. On some lakes, large trout eat small lamprey eels.

MAMMALS Trout and bass strike mice, shrews, and other small mammals that happen to fall in the water. Mouse imitations tied with buoyant deer hair are killers for large bass and big brown trout, which feed at night. Fish the fly on a strong leader close to overhanging banks, and manipulate it to simulate an animal struggling to escape. In Alaska, large rainbow trout nail lemmings, small rodents that migrate in large numbers—sometimes suicidally—across streams.

IN A NUTSHELL

1. Fish are predators as well as prey. As predators, they attack creatures that appear to be fleeing, crippled, or so abundant that the prey is easy to take without much effort.

2. To select an artificial fly that simulates a fish's natural food, determine what the fish is eating by observing it and collecting samples. Match the size, shape, and color of the natural food and animate your fly to make it look alive.

3. Attractor flies look nothing like natural insects, but they sometimes catch fish when nothing else will. To survive, fish must be curious about things that may be edible and nutritious; when a big, buggy-looking thing comes floating along, it often will provoke an opportunistic predator to strike.

5

WHERE TO FIND FISH

> **“**I began to scout up and down the shoreline in
> Manhattan on bright fall afternoons. At a
> rotted wooden pipe that had the appearance of
> a large barrel extending into the East River at
> Twentieth Street, I saw alewives nosing
> against moss-covered pilings. More bait
> appeared in the semi-clear water in sudden
> relief against the dark background of a
> drowned car seat.**”**
>
> **—IAN FRAZIER**
> “On Urban Shores” from *The New Yorker*

Finding fish on an unfamiliar piece of water is easy when you
look for the three things a fish needs to survive:

- Water that holds enough oxygen to breathe.
- A spot where the fish can get the most food for the least effort.
- A place to hide nearby.

To find freshwater fish, look for water clean and cool so it contains
oxygen and a lot of food—insects and baitfish—near an overhanging
bank or a tangle of brush, places where fish can hide from danger.

"Evening Breeze"—Rawlins Creek, Alaska.

Saltwater fish need similar conditions: Clean, oxygen-rich water, a place where the tides provide food, and cover—places where prey may be hiding. Marshes, tidal rivers, bays, and salt ponds are ideal. On open water, look for reefs, rockpiles, sand flats, and similar places where fish feed.

A pair of sunglasses with polarized lenses and a thermometer will help you find fish in shallow water.

First, assemble your gear and get your boots and vest on, but don't slip into the water right away. Instead, put a pair of polarized glasses over your eyes and wear a cap with a visor to shade your face. Then, quietly creep up to the bank. Crouch low or sneak through the brush; if there are fish in the water, they probably will not see you as long as you stay low.

HOW TO SEE FISH

When you locate a fishy-looking spot, your polarized glasses will help you find fish there. Don't look for the fish themselves, however, because they are well camouflaged, blending into their surroundings. Instead, watch the bottom and look for their shadows.

Remember to take your time, and before you slip into the water to start fishing, stay as still as a kingfisher as you watch the water.

Crouching midstream, or casting from a kneeling position for better concealment.

The polarized lenses of your glasses cut through the water's surface glare to help you spot fish. Here's what to look for:

SIGNS ON THE SURFACE

In the moving water of a river or a tidal flat, watch for fish feeding on or near the surface.

RINGS Trout, bass, and panfish create rings on the water when they rise to take insects off the surface. When you see rings appearing again and again in the same spot, you have found an actively feeding fish. Probably it is eating insects. You must watch the surface of the

The angler at left is too close, too erect, and too exposed. The angler at right is crouched, further away, and less exposed.

A trout's cone of vision.

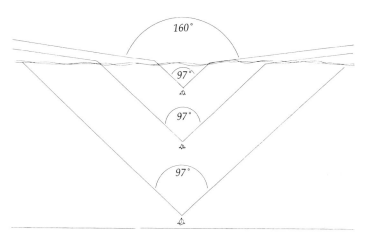

A trout's cone of vision remains constant at all depths: always 97°. The deeper a fish lies, the broader its cone of vision becomes—thus, the more it can see. At the surface, the fish's cone of vision compresses from 160° to 97°—because light striking the surface less than 10° above the horizon is reflected and does not enter the water.

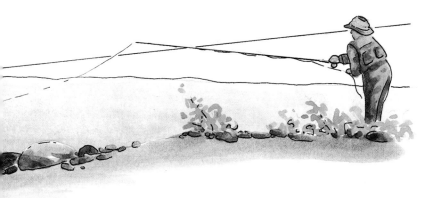

*Rings on the water's surface indicate that a
fish is rising to the surface to feed on insects.*

stream to determine what kinds of bugs the fish is eating so you can select a fly to simulate the real insects.

Occasionally, on some extremely rich streams, the insects on the
surface are so thick that trout and smallmouth bass poke their snouts
into the air and tread water in one place, as the current washes the
bugs into their mouths. At such times the fish are easy to spot.

SPLASHES If trout are splashing as they rise to the surface, they
probably are feeding on caddisflies. The insects pop from the water to
the air so quickly that the fish have to go into a high-speed chase to catch
them.

Bass splash as they strike dragonflies and damselflies hovering
just above the water's surface.

BULGES Frequently, trout and smallmouth bass grab insects just
beneath the surface as the bugs are about to emerge from the water and
into the air. Sometimes, even when adult mayflies blanket the top of the
water, the fish prefer to feed only inches below. When a trout or smallmouth is feeding on emerging insects just below the surface, the fish
makes the water bulge upward, and sometimes you may see the fish's
back and its top fin, the dorsal. Floating nymphs, soft-hackle flies, and
emerger patterns often fool such fish.

Splashes usually occur when fish are feeding on caddisflies. Bass will strike damselflies and dragonflies hovering just above the surface—and trout will sometimes take any fly by actually leaping out of the water.

Bulges on the surface suggest that trout and smallmouth bass are feeding just inches below the water's surface. Sometimes you'll see a fish's back and top fin when it is bulging.

Tailing: When fish feed on the bottom in shallow water, their tails sometimes extend above the surface. Bonefish, permit, and striped bass will tail as they hunt for crabs and other prey.

TAILING   When fish are feeding on the bottom in shallow water, their tails sometimes extend above the surface. You can spot bonefish, permit, and even striped bass tailing as they hunt for crabs and other food on the bottom.

WAKES, PUSHES, AND NERVOUS WATER   In the shape of a V on the surface, a wake reveals fish, too. On a stream, a wake usually means trouble. A fish senses a threat and is bolting for cover, creating the wake. The fish probably will not take a fly until it calms down and resumes feeding.

On ponds and tidal flats, however, a V-shaped wake often exposes a fish that is actively feeding, attacking prey in shallow water. Pike and pickerel charge out of their hiding spots to nail baitfish many yards away.

Bonefish, striped bass, and other saltwater fish also create wakes when they hunt prey in shallow water.

Sometimes, as fish slowly cruise over a tidal flat, they "push" water. The surface appears to be bulging and the bulge moves, revealing the fish's presence.

A northern pike and other fish will create wakes when they pursue a fly. Most frequently seen on ponds and tidal flats, a V-shaped wake suggests that a fish is actively attacking prey; but this occurs on trout streams, too.

In deeper water, schools of bluefish, bonito, and other predators make the water's surface look "nervous." On still days, nervous water has a tiny chop to it. On windy days, nervous water is harder to spot; look for areas on the surface that seem to be moving slower—or in a different direction—than the tide.

SENSORY FISHING

To enjoy fly fishing completely, use more than your sense of vision.

To find bluefish or striped bass along a beach, for example, try to find a spot where the air smells like cucumbers. That's how many experienced surf fishers describe the scent of menhaden—the baitfish—when bluefish and bass are attacking them.

When you're night fishing, listen for the popping sounds many fish make when they are feeding. Largemouth bass often splash when they attack prey. And a school of small baitfish sounds like rain when they all jump out of the water to escape a predator beneath the water.

An acute sense of touch will enable you to detect a bite when you are fishing flies beneath the surface. Develop sensitivity by having a friend simulate a fish, tugging your line ever so gently as you keep your eyes closed.

SLICKS   Sometimes, a shiny slick or calm spot on the water reveals the presence of schools of saltwater fish, especially bluefish, near the surface.

Motoring through a slick will frighten away fish; instead, slowly approach the edge, kill the motor, and drift on the wind or the current as you fish through a slick.

WHEN FISH AREN'T ON TOP

If you don't see fish through your polarized glasses, it's time to use another fish-finding tool: your thermometer.

Cold-blooded creatures, fish depend on the water around them to regulate their body temperature. When the water is very cold or very warm, fish tend to be inactive. They don't eat much, so they probably won't strike your fly.

In waters that are too warm or too cold, fish usually cannot find much food, so they have to hunt somewhere else.

When the water starts getting too cold, many fish will migrate to warmer waters. Saltwater fish such as striped bass and bluefish swim to southern waters every autumn. In a freshwater pond, fish go deep where the water is warmer in winter.

Water temperature also may tell you how much dissolved oxygen it contains—an important clue for finding fish, especially trout on a stream.

During the summer, when stream levels drop and water temperatures rise, there may not be enough oxygen in the water for fish to breathe.

Brown trout usually tolerate warmer water than rainbows or cutthroats. Brook trout and lake trout prefer much colder water. With rare exceptions, trout are most active when the water temperature is around fifty-eight or fifty-nine degrees Fahrenheit.

When the water is warmer than seventy degrees, use your thermometer to search for cooler spots. Trout often migrate to springs and to the mouths of little feeder streams where the water is cooler and there is more oxygen.

In ponds, coldwater fish such as northern pike and smallmouth bass usually prowl shallow water right after the ice melts. When summer arrives and the pond warms up, they either move to deep water or congregate at the mouth of a cool inlet stream.

Though largemouth bass prefer very warm water, they tend to stay on the bottom or beneath shady lily pads during the day. When the water's surface is cooler, early in the morning and late in the evening, largemouths come to the top to feed.

To find spots where fish are most likely to take a fly, refer to the following chart of preferred feeding temperatures.

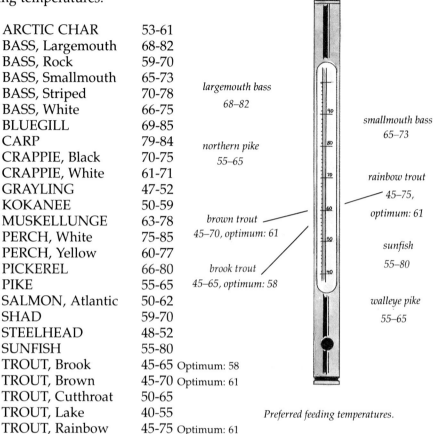

ARCTIC CHAR	53-61
BASS, Largemouth	68-82
BASS, Rock	59-70
BASS, Smallmouth	65-73
BASS, Striped	70-78
BASS, White	66-75
BLUEGILL	69-85
CARP	79-84
CRAPPIE, Black	70-75
CRAPPIE, White	61-71
GRAYLING	47-52
KOKANEE	50-59
MUSKELLUNGE	63-78
PERCH, White	75-85
PERCH, Yellow	60-77
PICKEREL	66-80
PIKE	55-65
SALMON, Atlantic	50-62
SHAD	59-70
STEELHEAD	48-52
SUNFISH	55-80
TROUT, Brook	45-65 Optimum: 58
TROUT, Brown	45-70 Optimum: 61
TROUT, Cutthroat	50-65
TROUT, Lake	40-55
TROUT, Rainbow	45-75 Optimum: 61

largemouth bass
68–82

smallmouth bass
65–73

northern pike
55–65

rainbow trout
45–75,
optimum: 61

brown trout
45–70, optimum: 61

sunfish
55–80

brook trout
45–65, optimum: 58

walleye pike
55–65

Preferred feeding temperatures.

FINDING FISH IN FLOWING WATER

In flowing water, fish face upstream. With their mouths in the current, they can catch bits of food—mostly insects and baitfish—caught in the water's flow.

Swimming against the current, however, burns a lot of the fish's energy, so it needs a lot of food, the fuel to maintain that energy.

To survive, a fish must take in more fuel than it burns.

In a stream, fish stay in spots where the current brings plenty of food, but where the water flow is not so strong that the fish will burn too much energy. Also, fish need a hiding place nearby, in case they sense danger from above the water.

To find fish, look for spots where the stream's normal current is broken. Fish lie on the slower side of the break. There is enough current to carry food to the fish, but staying in the slower flow does not require too much energy. If there is a place to hide nearby, the spot where the current breaks is even more attractive to fish.

BREAKS AND EDGES IN THE CURRENT

Fish often stay in "pockets" behind large rocks, which break the current and sweep food to them. To find submerged rocks, watch for bulges in the stream and for small patches of water that look slick against the rest of the current.

Trout lies in a spring creek.
A   weedbed channels
B   overhanging banks
C   springs
D   bank vegetation
E   riffles
F   eddy
G   run
H   slough

Sometimes, on slow-flowing streams, fish stay in front of rocks where the flow has created a depression on the bottom to break the current. On faster streams, clusters of rocks often form funnels that carry food to fish waiting downstream on the edges of the fast current.

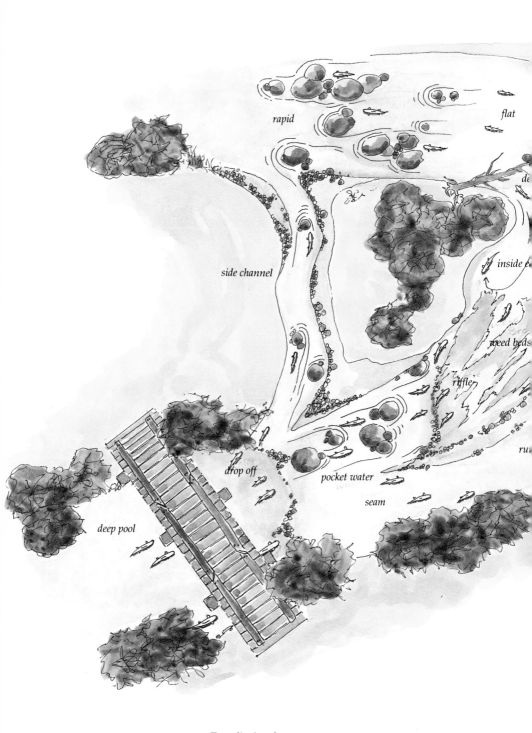

rapid

flat

side channel

inside e

weed beds

riffle

ru

drop off

pocket water

seam

deep pool

Trout lies in a freestone stream.

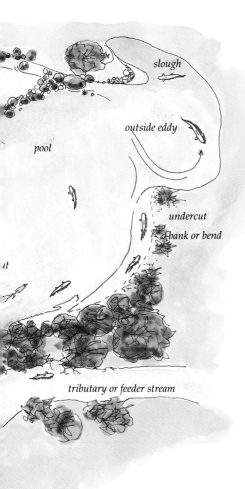

slough

outside eddy

pool

undercut
bank or bend

ut

tributary or feeder stream

Here are a few more clues to help you find fish in flowing water:

DEADFALLS Trees that have fallen into the water create ideal places for fish to stay. The branches not only break the current, but they provide a place for the fish to hide.

BRUSHY BANKS Like deadfalls, banks overgrown with grass or brush create a hiding place for fish and, during the summer, the vegetation drips with ants, grasshoppers, and other insects for the fish to eat. Especially good places for trout are muddy banks that hang over a stream.

POOLS Deep, slow, and wide, pools generally hold most fish in the middle where a lot of food sweeps down on easy currents.

The beginning of the pool, or "head," holds some fish, usually behind rocks, but there usually are more fish farther down the pool.

Fish also stay on a pool's edges, where two currents meet. Such an edge is called a "seam" and it looks like a line on the water; fish generally stay on the slower side of the seam.

The "tail," or lower end of a pool, where the water starts to become shallow, often holds large fish behind rocks and near the spot where the water quickly changes from deep to shallow.

On small streams, a log or row of stones cutting across the tail of a pool is called a "lip." Trout generally stay in front of the lip catching food before it washes over the edge.

RIFFLES Shallow, choppy water generally downstream of deep, slow pools, riffles usually hold fish, but there are fewer of them and they are smaller than the pool's fish. At the top and the middle of a riffle, look for patches of smooth water that reveal depressions deep enough to hold fish. At the bottom of a riffle, look for a "chute" that resembles a funnel carrying food to fish waiting on the edge where the current is slower than in the middle.

BENDS On deep, winding streams, fish usually stay on the inside of a bend where the water is slower, so they don't have to use as much energy as they would in faster currents.

When a shallow stream bends, look for fish on the outside of the turn where the current makes the water deeper. The deeper cut funnels food to the fish waiting near the edge.

EDDIES When the current cuts into a bank, it creates an eddy, an indentation where the water swirls back on itself, moving opposite the main current. The eddy's swirling water gathers food and attracts fish. Because the currents are flowing against the main current, however, fishing an eddy may be tricky or even downright difficult.

SIDE CHANNELS Created by floods and dug deeper by currents, a side channel is like a small stream that breaks away from the main river and then rejoins it. The current generally is slower than in the main stream and the food abundant—good conditions for larger fish that cannot afford to waste energy.

WEED BEDS On spring creeks where watercress or other weeds blanket the streambed, currents cut channels in the sandy bottom. Trout hug the edges of the channels, tight against the weeds, where there is plenty of food and a quick place to hide.

Remember: Fish find places where there is enough oxygen to breathe and where they can get the most food for the least effort, with a hiding spot nearby. You may not find fish in the same spots each day, however. A stream is always changing; before you start fishing, invest some time watching the water.

FINDING FISH IN PONDS AND LAKES

In still waters, fish don't have to burn energy fighting a current, so they can afford to cruise in search of food. Sometimes they prowl a pond hunting for prey. More often, however, fish stay close to a dependable food source where hunting does not require too much effort. A place to hide nearby also is important when larger predators threaten.

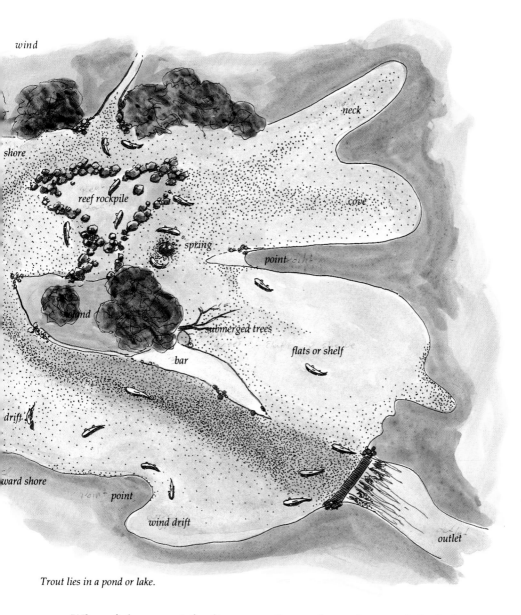

Trout lies in a pond or lake.

When fish are not feeding near the surface of a pond, look for them in the following spots:

FEEDER STREAMS   Also called "inlets," feeder streams pour food and cool water with a lot of fresh oxygen into a pond or lake. Fish often congregate at the stream's mouth to feed. During the summer, they stay at the mouth and sometimes swim into the stream to stay cool and breathe easily.

ROCKS Rocks shelter crayfish, minnows, and many insects that gamefish eat. In cold weather, exposed rocks on the northern shore of a pond soak up sunlight to warm the water around them and attract fish.

SUBMERGED STRUCTURES Rock piles, trees, and brush, submerged beneath the surface, attract baitfish and larger predatory fish looking for a lot of food with little effort.

DROP-OFFS Before and after a cold front moves into an area—when the barometric pressure and water temperature change quickly—fish often hug steep drop-offs along a pond's bottom. With minimal effort, they can rise and descend along the drop-off to hunt for food.

SHADE Trees, docks, and bridges all offer shade in which bass and other warmwater fish find food and protection from the summer sun. Trees and overhanging brush also spill such insects as ants and inchworms into the water to attract trout.

WEED BEDS Patches of water lilies, cattails, and other aquatic plants provide gamefish with food, protection from other predators, and shade. On trout ponds, look for fish on the edges. On bass ponds, start fishing on the edge of a weed bed, and then work poppers and other snag-proof surface flies over the top of the weeds.

SHELVES The shallow and narrow edges of deep alpine lakes produce insects in the oxygen-rich water where trout cruise, searching for food.

THE ONE-HOUR FISHING FIX

The best time to go fly fishing is anytime. You don't need a weekend or even a whole day to have fun and improve your skills.

An hour, whenever you can find one, is plenty of time to relax with your fly tackle. Ask your local fly-fishing dealer about ponds and streams near your home, places where you can catch panfish, bass, or trout.

A couple of times a week, invest an hour or so fishing there. Soon, your casting and fishing skills will improve and immediately you will feel happier and more relaxed.

FISH ON SALTWATER ESTUARIES AND FLATS

Saltwater fish have the same needs as freshwater fish but their surroundings change continually as tides rise and fall.

Rich with baitfish, shrimp, and other prey, estuaries attract gamefish. In tidal rivers and coastal waterways, such fish as sea-run trout and striped bass hunt prey in many of the same spots where you would find fish on a freshwater stream.

Along the Gulf of Mexico and the Atlantic coasts, redfish, bonefish, and many other predators also prowl tidal flats in bays, salt ponds, or lagoons and around islands as they hunt for food.

When fish aren't pushing water or showing their tails as they feed, look for them in the following spots.

THE EDGE OF THE FLAT On a falling tide, fish often stay just off the edge of a flat in deeper water, waiting for the current to wash food over the edge to them. In a bay, the fish may be in the channel running alongside a flat at low tide.

OVERHANGING BANKS AND BENDS In coastal streams, sea-run trout, striped bass, and other gamefish often use overhanging mud banks and bends as freshwater trout do, attacking baitfish and eating shrimp washed down in the current.

CREEK MOUTHS Like freshwater feeder streams, the mouths of tidal creeks pour fresh food into an estuary. Fish stake out creek mouths to intercept prey as the tide falls.

RIPS When water pours out of a river or a channel and meets the incoming tide, it creates a rip, a stretch of turbulent water near the mouth. Fish work the edge of the rip, where the current is not as strong, and wait for the turbulence to wash baitfish, shrimp, and other prey to them.

MARSH CHANNELS These are tiny canals, cut to drain marshes where hay once grew; fish are attracted to the mouths of channels, where they empty into the main stream.

One of the easiest ways to find fish on salt water is to watch for flocks of gulls and terns diving madly on the surface. Chances are, a school of game fish is herding bait to the top where the little fish are easy pickings for the birds.

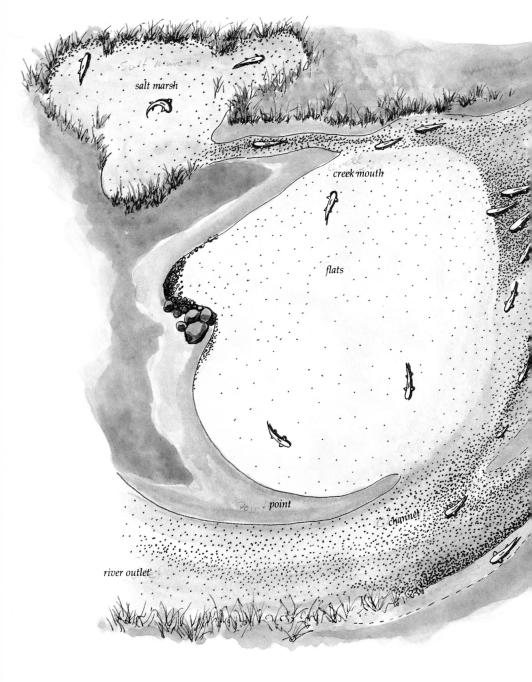

salt marsh

creek mouth

flats

point

channel

river outlet

Finding fish in a saltwater estuary.

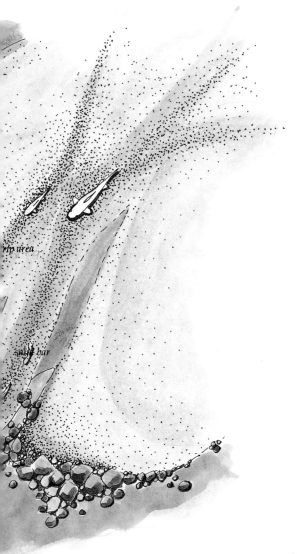

rip area

sand bar

IN A NUTSHELL
. . . .

1. Fish find places where there is enough oxygen to breathe and where they can get the most food for the least effort, with a hiding spot nearby.

2. In flowing water, fish find spots where there is a break in the current—behind rocks, on the slower side of converging currents, and in side channels.

3. The most valuable tools for finding fish on a stream are polarized sunglasses, a thermometer, and patience.

6

TACTICS TO MAKE YOUR FLIES LOOK ALIVE

"Flailers share one thing in common: They rarely raise, much less ever catch, a trout. Watching one at his devotionals swiftly reveals why. After resolutely stomping up to the water he will so shortly rid of all trout, your typical flailer strips out line like an overworked barber whipping up a cold lather. Then suddenly he braces himself and lifts the accumulated mass and blindly flings it out yonder as far as he can. Then, before his fly has fairly landed, he retrieves the whole whirling mess and whales her out again. This goes on all day.**"**

—ROBERT TRAVER
Trout Magic

To catch fish, you must animate an artificial fly so it appears to be alive—or let it float "dead drift," if that's how fish would find it.

Sometimes, you make a fly appear as though it is swimming or crawling or fleeing. When you're fishing a floating mayfly imitation, however, it has to behave like all the other mayflies caught in the current, drifting with no unusual movement.

Fish in a stream station themselves in spots where the water acts like a conveyor belt, delivering oxygen to breathe and insects and other animals to eat. Sometimes a fish will experiment, eating an unusual item such as a twig or a seed, as long as that item is drifting along naturally. Watching hundreds of possible food items drifting by, a fish becomes accustomed to seeing things come along a certain path at a certain speed. When it detects any unusual movement in a possible food item, the fish either ignores it or perceives it as a threat and flees.

The unusual or unnatural movement of an artificial fly in current is called "drag." Sometimes the wind causes drag but the usual causes are water currents, pushing or pulling on your fly line and leader. They make the artificial fly drift slower, faster, or along a different path from real insects in the current.

Drag often creates a V-shaped wake behind a floating fly. The easiest way to detect drag, however, is to compare your fly's drift with the drift of a living insect or a fleck of foam next to it. If your fly is floating slower or faster than an object beside it, drag has set in.

If you are convinced that your artificial fly matches the size, shape, and color of living insects on the stream, but fish keep ignoring it, your leader tippet may be too thick or, more likely, drag has taken over, making the fly appear unnatural.

You have several options for eliminating drag. The idea is to eliminate the effect of current between you and your fly.

CHANGE YOUR POSITION   The best way to eliminate drag is to move and eliminate the currents between you and your fly.

If you are casting to a fish feeding at the surface, you can get closer to it than if it were in deeper water. The higher the fish is feeding, the less it can see above the surface. Approach the fish slowly and quietly, like a heron.

HUNT LIKE A HERON

Your first five or ten minutes on a new piece of water are key to finding fish there.

As you kneel on the bank, pretend that you are a kingfisher or an eagle, and observe the water as a predator. Don't make a move until you are reasonably certain that you've spotted a fish—or a place where a fish is feeding. Take your time. Stay still.

When you do enter the water, walk like a heron. Take your time as you get into position. Walk slowly so your legs don't create ripples on the water. Stay low.

Fly rodding is as much hunting as it is fishing. Learn how to be better at the game by studying a heron on the hunt.

If you can, try positioning yourself directly above the fish in the current. Feed your fly to the fish by pulling fly line off your reel and wiggling the rod tip close to the water surface so the line pays out. Positioning yourself directly above the fish allows you to control your fly as you would a puppet.

DAPPING   is an ancient and deadly fly-fishing technique invented when fly fishers used long poles with a length of line too short to cast. Dapping eliminates drag altogether because there is no line on the water, only a little leader and the fly.

On a stream, dapping works on fish feeding next to the bank. The idea is to stalk the fish, usually by crawling, to get right next to it without it seeing you. Delicately lower the fly just above the fish so it drifts directly to the fish.

Dapping also is an effective method for animating an artificial caddisfly to make it appear as though it is dropping to the surface, laying eggs. Work the fly like a yo-yo just up-current of a fish.

Though dapping may be considered an unethical fishing technique in some places, it requires great skill as a stalker.

CHANGE YOUR TIPPET   Sometimes adding a longer, finer piece of tippet between your leader and fly helps to eliminate drag. At the end of your cast, a long, flimsy tippet tends to pile up on the water. The current still pushes and pulls on it, but by the time the currents straighten it to affect the fly, a fish may strike.

CAST SOME S-CURVES   Making your fly line zigzag on the water will give your fly more time to float before the current seizes the line and pulls the fly unnaturally.

The moment *after* you snap-STOP your forward cast, wiggle the rod tip from side to side as you lower it to the water. As the fly line falls to the water, it will take on a series of S-curves that will help to delay drag.

MEND THE LINE   "Mending" is a technique for prolonging a fly's drift by throwing a bow into the fly line. It absorbs the current's push so the water cannot straighten the line too quickly and make the fly drag.

A simple mend works like this: When the water starts to push your fly line into an arc down-current, point the rod tip at the arc, then flip your forearm and wrist up-current. The motion is like flipping a page of a large book.

You also may mend your line in the air with a "reach cast." When you feel comfortable with the four-part cast, try it: After the snap-STOP of the forward cast, quickly reach your casting arm far to the side. The

An upstream mend: To roll the line upstream, point the rod tip at the arc and flip your forearm and wrist up-current—like you're flipping a page of a large book.

An upstream mend completed: Slack line on the water ensures a drag-free drift.

fly will go to the target where the rod tip was pointing when you stopped the stroke. The fly line, however, will land to the side. When you're fishing on a stream, reaching up-current will give the fly more time to drift without drag before the flow pulls on the line.

ANIMATING FLIES

Dapping an imitation caddisfly, bouncing it on the surface as though it were laying eggs, can drive an ordinarily lethargic fish into a fit of aggression. There are many other techniques to animate artificial flies so they behave as as though they were alive.

Animating nymphs and pupae: Just as your imitation reaches the fish, lift your fly as though it were swimming to the surface to emerge as an adult.

Jigging a Woolly Bugger: Lift and lower your rod tip as you retrieve line a little at a time, so that the fly makes short hops on the bottom.

LIFTING NYMPHS AND PUPAE   To simulate a mayfly or caddisfly about to emerge, cast your imitation in the current above a fish you can see. Cast it far enough up-current so it has time to sink to the fish's level. Watch your strike indicator to keep track of the fly's position, and just as it reaches the fish, lift the fly as though it were swimming to the surface to emerge as an adult. Often, the lift will stimulate the fish to follow the fly and strike.

JIGGING   Many flies, like the Woolly Bugger and the Clouser Minnow, are made of materials that undulate and pulsate as they hop along the bottom. The Clouser Minnow already has weight built in, so it is ideal for jigging; with other flies add a split-shot weight to the leader, next to the fly's nose. Cast across the current, and as the fly sweeps down, lift and lower your rod tip as you retrieve line a little at a time, so the fly makes short hops on the bottom. The motion simulates a crayfish or a baitfish.

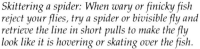

Skittering a spider: When wary or finicky fish reject your flies, try a spider or bivisible fly and retrieve the line in short pulls to make the fly look like it is hovering or skating over the fish.

Swimming the streamer: Keep your rod tip low to the water or just beneath the surface and use your line hand to pull the line in brief bursts.

SKATING OR SKITTERING   On heavily fished streams, wary fish may reject even the most realistic, drag-free flies. When you encounter such finicky fish, try a bushy Spider or Bivisible fly. Cast it up and across the current, then lift your rod tip high to keep line off the water. With your line hand, retrieve line in short pulls to make the fly appear as though it is hovering or skating just above the reluctant fish.

SWIMMING   Take the time to watch minnows in the water: They dart about in brief bursts, making longer bursts when they sense danger. Often their flight triggers predatory fish to strike. To make an artificial baitfish appear to be alive, cast the fly across and slightly down-current; keep your rod tip low to the water or just beneath the surface, and use your line hand to pull the line in brief bursts.

To make the fly swim very fast, so it appears to be fleeing, mend the line *downstream* so the current makes the fly rush down and across the stream.

Popping a hopper: To create a popping sound as you retrieve a fly, keep your rod parallel to the water's surface and use your line hand to make snappy pulls.

A bass popper, designed with a cupped head, should also be retrieved with a low rod and short, sharp pulls.

Never swim a fly toward a fish; it will appear as though it is attacking.

POPPING Many flies make a popping or gurgling sound as you retrieve them, to attract bass, bluefish, and many other kinds of gamefish. Popping such lures as the Goofus Bug, a popular Maine fly, attracts even wary trout. To get the most volume from a popper, keep your rod parallel to the water and use the wrist of your line hand to make short, snappy pulls.

SPLASHING Practicing the four-part cast, you have been concentrating on making the fly, leader, and line flutter gently to the water. In your fishing, however, you may encounter situations where making the fly splash will attract a fish's attention. Largemouth bass are especially attracted to a big bug making a splat on the surface. A similar noise attracts big brown trout at night. Drive a cast downward to make the fly splash, but stop the rod tip high enough to prevent the line from crashing down and frightening fish.

IN A NUTSHELL

1. To catch fish, artificial flies must behave as though they are alive.

2. When water currents straighten your line and leader, "drag" will make your floating fly behave unnaturally and fish will ignore it.

3. Most underwater flies and many surface flies are more effective when you animate them to behave as though they are alive.

7

HOOKING AND FIGHTING FISH

*"Out of the water he rose like a rocket—out and out,
and still there was more to him, no end to him.
More bird than fish he seemed as he hovered
above the water, his spots and spangles patterned
like plumage. I half expected to see his sides
unfold and spread in flight, as though, like the
insects he fed upon, he had undergone metamorphosis
and hatched. His gleaming wetness gave an
iridescent glaze to him, and as he rose into the
sunshine his multitudinous markings sparkled
as though he were studded with jewels."*

—WILLIAM HUMPHREY
My Moby Dick

Luring a fish to strike your artificial fly is the object of this sport. But what do you do when a fish does strike? How do you hook it? And then what?

Relax. Just about everyone's First-Fish-on-a-Fly-Rod hooks itself. A gift.

To catch your second fish, however, requires some concentration. If you are fishing a floating fly, you must keep your eyes on it. If the fly

Sneaking up on fish.

is beneath the surface, you must remove as much slack from the line as you can, and feel for the slightest twitch. Or concentrate on your floating strike indicator to signal a bite; when a fish takes the fly in flowing water, the strike indicator bobs or hesitates briefly and you must react immediately before the fish spits the fly.

FLOATING FLIES

Reacting *too* quickly is probably the main reason fly fishers lose fish on floating flies. Seeing a trout rise to your dry fly or a bass attack your popper is so exciting that you may lift the rod tip and pull the fly right out of the fish's mouth.

Relax. Let the fish strike, and only after the fly disappears should you strike back.

If you sharpened the hook and squeezed down the barb, the fish may hook itself. To be certain, lift the rod tip up and to your side to tighten the line between you and the fish. On the initial strike, handle the rod with force.

To strike a bass or pike, increase the amount of force by tugging at the line with one hand as you lift the rod tip with the other. Just be sure that the fish has taken the fly before you strike.

WATCH A CAT TO LEARN ABOUT FISH

When you're fishing a surface bug such as a popper, diver, or slider, imagine that you're teasing a kitten with a length of string.

Bass, northern pike, and some saltwater gamefish react to erratic, stop-and-go retrieves as a kitten responds to a piece of string moving across the floor. Prepared to pounce, a kitten doesn't budge as long as the lure is moving steadily within its attack zone.

The predator lunges as soon as the lure appears to be escaping from its attack zone, or when the prey appears to be vulnerable—when it moves in jerks, as though it is injured.

SINKING FLIES

On streams, the water flow often sets the hook on a fish that has taken your streamer fly.

Fishing a nymph is another story. Many fly fishers miss fish because they aren't aware of the bite. A strike indicator helps, but you must pay close attention to it. The moment the indicator pauses or bobs, you must strike. Because the water flow creates a lot of slack, you must strike quickly and hard, lifting the rod high and to the side, and pulling the line with your other hand. When you are fishing a sinking fly on a pond or in salt water, you may feel the bite while you are animating the fly, but often the fish hits the moment you pause, when the line is slack. If you fish with your rod tip just beneath the surface, you may detect the bite, but doing so takes a lot of practice. To develop your skill, fish artificial nymphs for sunfish.

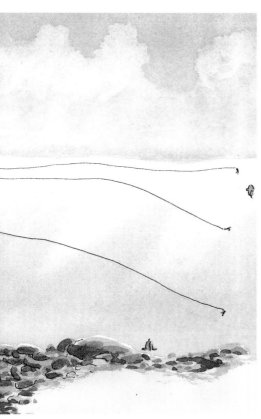

Fly line densities will affect the buoyancy of your fly. Fish will also strike at different stages: fish may hit when your line is slack, for example.

RESTING THE WATER

Trout and most other fish have a wide field of view from the front to both sides of their bodies, and a blind spot directly behind them. However, even when you position yourself in the water directly behind a fish, it probably can sense your presence, and if the fish senses that you are a threat, it is going to bolt.

Whenever you can, cast from shore and stay low.

If you must enter the water to position yourself for a cast, wade slowly—a step at a time—until you reach your spot. Then relax, and allow the fish to become accustomed to you.

If the fish behave warily and do leave a pool, get out of the water and out of sight. Devise another approach and let the pool "rest" as the fish return.

FIGHTING FISH

As ethical anglers, we are obliged to use the heaviest possible tackle to land fish quickly without exhausting them to death.

A hooked fish is fighting for its life; it will jump, run, dive, and wear itself out. Your job is to subdue it and to release it as quickly as possible, or to kill it immediately if you are going to eat it.

As soon as you hook a fish, it is going to run. Control the line with your rod hand's middle finger against the grip. Keep the line tight between you and the fish.

If there is any loose line on the water or in your boat, let the fish pull it out, or crank it onto the reel as soon as you can.

"Pump" the rod to bring the fish in. Lift the rod tip to pull the fish closer. Then quickly reel in the line you have gained as you lower the rod tip toward the fish again. Lift the rod tip again to bring the fish closer, and continue the pumping action.

If the fish jumps, "bow" to it: Quickly lean forward and stab the rod tip toward the fish to give it some momentary slack for its jump.

If the fish "bulldogs" you, shaking its head and refusing to budge, lower the rod tip to the water's surface and work it from side to side, reeling as you gain line.

When a fish such as a largemouth bass wraps the leader around weeds and you cannot get to the fish to unwrap the line, sometimes the fish will swim out of the snag if you feed it plenty of slack line. Other times, it will spit the fly.

When you're fishing from a boat and you hook an uncontrollable trophy fish, engage the motor and chase the fish.

If a hooked fish swims under the boat, be sure the propeller is disengaged and poke the rod tip into the water to "walk" the line to the other side and regain control. Be very careful, however, not to let the rod touch the hull, which could snap it.

LANDING FISH

When you have a fish under control, reel in enough line so you can reach out to the fish. Keep the rod tip high.

Please avoid touching a fish you are going to release. Removing its body slime makes it vulnerable to disease. And please do not remove it from the water; its internal organs don't handle gravity very well.

If your fish is small, slide your hand down the leader, grasp the barbless hook, and twist it free. If your fly is deep in the fish's mouth, you may try using a pair of pliers or forceps to retrieve it, but it's probably more prudent to snip the leader near the fish's mouth and let it swim free; the hook probably will corrode away.

To subdue larger fish that you plan to release, use a net made of soft material that will not hurt the fish, and keep it in the water if you can.

If you must handle a fish that you plan to release, please wet your hands first to reduce damage to its protective slime.

If you hook its gills, a fish will die soon. Ethically, you are obliged to kill it and eat it. If you are fishing on waters posted for catch-and-release fishing, you face an ethical dilemma: Allowing the fish to sink and die is a sinful waste, but the law requires that you release the dying fish while it is still alive.

When you kill a fish to eat, do it quickly: With a club (anglers call it a "priest") or a stone, sharply strike the top of its head.

Then care for it properly to maintain maximum table quality. Bleed a saltwater fish by cutting off its tail. Remove its entrails and gills as soon as possible. Gut a shark immediately to prevent an ammonia-like flavor from developing. Store dead fish on ice until you return to port.

Please do not hang living freshwater fish on a stringer, where they will die slowly. If you plan to eat a fish, kill it quickly, gut it immediately, and store it on ice. If you store freshwater fish in a creel, use one made of cloth that you can soak. As the water evaporates it keeps the fish cool. Line a wicker creel with thick layers of ferns and grasses to insulate gutted fish and keep them cool.

If you enjoy eating the fish you catch, invest in a good cookbook so you can prepare them in a variety of ways.

And please remember to limit your catch rather than catch your limit.

RULES OF
THE ROAD

"The ethics of sportsmanship is not a fixed code, but must be formulated and practiced by the individual, with no referee but the Almighty."

—ALDO LEOPOLD
in "Goose Music" from *Round River*

As short as this chapter is, it could be distilled to a single sentence: Treat other anglers, your surroundings, and your fish with respect.

Throughout this handbook, we encourage you to relax. Fly fishing is your door to leave the competition of everyday life and to enter a natural world where two gentle people can enjoy being together while respecting one another's privacy and need for solitude.

With strangers we share stories and flies, but never a stretch of stream without first asking permission.

Even public waters?

Especially public waters. As streams, lakes, and ocean beaches become more crowded, it becomes more important to practice the Golden Rule and some commonsense rules of the road:

- If someone is fishing a pool, wait until the other angler is out of the water or find another spot for yourself. If you come across a fisher who is sitting on the bank next to a pool, he may be "resting" the water, allowing the fish there to resume feeding after they have been disturbed; before you enter the water, ask the other angler if you may fish there.

• We fish for different reasons. Some of us go fly fishing simply to catch some solitude. When you greet another fly fisher on the water, it's all right to ask, "How's the fishing?" If the other angler mumbles a response and looks away, respect that person's need for privacy and move along.

• Don't whoop when you hook a fish. It's boorish and stupid.

• Never cross a stream where another angler is fishing; instead, find a place to cross where you will not disturb him.

• When two fishers meet on a stream, and one is casting up-current while the other is casting down-current, the angler moving up-current has the right of way.

• On a large lake or the ocean, never cut between another boat and a school of fish or a sand flat that the other boat is working.

• Keep your distance from another angler whose boat is following a hooked fish.

• When another fisher shows you a secret fishing spot, never return alone without first asking your friend's permission. And never show the spot to anyone else.

• Don't build fires in the woods unless it's a matter of survival.

• Never cross private property without first asking permission, even when it is legal to do so.

• Pick up trash, even when it's not yours.

• When you clip off any kind of fishing line, put the waste in your pocket and dispose of it at home.

• Close all gates behind you, but don't lock gates that were unlocked when you arrived.

• Walk around, not through, livestock corrals and planted fields.

• Use the heaviest possible leader you can to subdue a fish quickly, without exhausting it.

• If you can, release a fish without touching it. And always use barbless hooks.

• Never transfer a fish from one pond to another.

• When you kill a fish to eat, kill it quickly and keep it properly. Gut it, bleed it, and store it in ice.

• Kill only enough fish to eat immediately. It's a good conservation practice, and besides, frozen fish tastes lousy.

• Tread gently as you wade so you do not disrupt the stream bottom. And replace rocks you've removed to examine for insects.

• Read your home state's fishing regulations before the start of each season. When you're fishing in another state or country, study the regulations as soon as you arrive there.

• Tip your fishing guide with cash. Inviting the guide to dinner is not a fair reward for showing you a great day of fishing, no matter how expensive the dinner may be. Guiding is a business. Dinner does not pay the guide's rent or buy groceries. Besides, at the end of a long work day, your guide probably wants to go home and relax. Fifteen to twenty percent is a good guideline.

• On a charter boat, tip the mate directly rather than including the tip in a single check to the skipper.

• Treat your guide like a friend, not an employee. Sure, it's his job to hold the boat steady in a thirty-knot wind, but don't expect him to hold it there forever. Take his advice about flies and techniques; he knows what works on the water you're fishing. At holidays, send him a greeting card.

• Don't look through your guide's gear or his fly boxes without permission.

• When you're fishing as a guest aboard a friend's boat, offer to bring lunch and beverages, and to pay for the fuel.

• When you discover which artificial flies are catching fish, share the information—and the flies—with other anglers.

• When another angler gives you a fly, open your box and invite him to take one of yours.

Fishing is one of the greatest gifts you can share.

• Join a conservation organization dedicated to buying and protecting water and land that support fish and wildlife. Loss of habitat to developers threatens our natural resources.

• Join a fishing club where you can improve your skills and share what you have learned.

• Invite someone less fortunate to go fishing. It's the greatest gift you can give yourself.

• Don't count fish or compete with other anglers. For some of us, the measure of success is getting a fish to strike; for others, success is making a good cast, or simply the sight of an osprey soaring.

9

FISH FOR THE FLY ROD

> ❝We take it slow and easy. We like to paddle a
> canoe or a float tube around the rim of a bass
> pond and cast bugs toward shore. We make a
> couple of Cape Cod bluefish-on-a-fly-rod runs
> each summer. We wade the Indianhead for
> shad in May. Sometimes we bring a sack of
> bluegills home from Bare Hill Pond. We filet
> them together while sharing a bottle of decent
> Chardonnay, and Andy deep fries them and
> we gorge on them the same night with
> another Chardonnay.❞
>
> **—WILLIAM G. TAPPLY**
> Opening Day and Other Neuroses

With your fly rod, you can catch fish all over the world. Here
are some of the gamefish you may find close to home and some tips on
how to catch them.

ATLANTIC SALMON The king of fly-rod fish, the Atlantic salmon
has a devoted following of anglers in North America and Europe. Un-

Atlantic Salmon

like Pacific salmon, Atlantic salmon can spawn more than once. At sea, the fish stores enough energy to return to its native stream, to climb waterfalls and to spawn without the need to eat. When a fish strikes a fly, it may be a simple reflex rather than a need to eat or to protect its territory. Fly fishers use a variety of long-established dry- and wet-fly techniques for catching Atlantic salmon. A hooked fish usually jumps several feet above the water in a majestic display of strength. Its population destroyed by dams and pollution, the Atlantic salmon is the object of an international restoration effort in North America.

BARRACUDA This toothy tropical saltwater fish strikes artificial flies with speed and power, and its first run against the reel is quick and desperate. Barracuda often prowl the same flats as bonefish, but they also hunt on reefs, among mangrove tangles, and near bridges and boat docks. The great barracuda of the Atlantic grows to over 100 pounds, but fish between three and fifty pounds are more common. Fished on wire shock tippets to resist abrasion, barracuda flies are slender and as long as ten inches, simulating needlefish. Realistic baitfish colors, such as blue and white, work well on barracuda flies, but the fish often seem to prefer fluorescent colors. You must retrieve the fly as quickly as possible to provoke a strike.

BASS Largemouth, smallmouth, and spotted bass sometimes slam bass bugs recklessly; at other times, bass can be as finicky as the most choosy trout. In streams, smallmouths and spotted bass are especially selective during large hatches of aquatic insects. The fish key in on the predominant food source and reject artificial flies that do not match the size, color, and behavior of the natural insects. Like large trout, however, selective smallmouths often will whack a streamer intruding into the bass's territory.

Largemouth bass attack almost anything that invades their territory including snakes, mice, birds, and frogs. Mostly, largemouths eat minnows and and other small fish. After spawning in the spring,

Largemouth bass attack a variety of prey: minnows, snakes, mice, birds, and frogs.

males guard the nest against salamanders, snakes, and other fish—such as carp and sunfish—which prey on bass eggs and young fish. Even after the young have left the nest, adult bass remain aggressive toward salamanders, snakes, and sunfish—and toward artificial flies simulating those creatures.

Poppers, divers, and sliders—bass bugs fished on or near the water's surface—offer the most excitement because you can see the raw violence of a predator striking prey.

BLUEFISH   From Florida to the Gulf of Maine, bluefish slash at flies resembling fish trying to escape. Whether they are young, six- to twelve-inch "skipjack" or "snapper" blues, slightly larger "cocktail" or "tailor" blues, or 20-pound "slammers," bluefish use their extraordinarily sharp teeth and powerful jaws to chop their prey into bits. During a feeding frenzy, a school of bluefish can make the water look as though it's boiling with the blood of baitfish. Menhaden and butterfish are especially vulnerable to bluefish attacks. Saltwater streamers and poppers simulating silver-and-white baitfish attract bluefish. Attach them with wire or a braided material that will withstand the bluefish's teeth. Bluefish apparently are subject to huge fluctuations in population size; when they are abundant, blues offer great sport, and they taste delicious.

BONEFISH These turbo-charged bottom feeders work shallow flats where wading fly fishers cast to fish they can see. Even small school fish tear line off the reel, but larger bonefish make a full spool of line melt off the reel in seconds. Foraging in tropical seas in the Northern and Southern Hemispheres, bonefish weighing over 20 pounds have been caught on bait in deep water but, typically, they are much smaller on the flats. Bonefish flies generally simulate shrimp and other creatures that live in turtle grass near the bottom in shallow water. American fly fishers release most of the bonefish they catch; in other parts of the world, however, the fish and its eggs are considered to be delectable.

BONITO Members of the mackerel family, these iridescent torpedoes nail a variety of flies that simulate rocket-powered baitfish. Because bonito move at such high speeds, casting to a school is useless; in the second it takes for your fly line to straighten out, the fish are gone. Casting for bonito is like shooting at flying targets: You have to lead the school, casting far ahead of the fish. When the fly lands, tuck the rod under your arm and retrieve the fly by stripping line hand-over-hand as quickly as you can. When a fish takes the fly, a sharp hook will set itself as the fish begins its run.

CARP Sharp-eyed and wary, carp are brutes when hooked. Intent on not becoming an ingredient in gefilte fish, hooked carp use power rather than speed to escape. Primarily vegetarians, they do eat a variety of creatures that live on the bottom and will take such flies as Woolly Worms and crayfish simulators. When mulberries are falling on a slow, warm stream, carp will rise to the surface to take a berry or a clipped deer-hair fly that looks like one.

CATFISH Bottom dwellers that taste delicious, catfish and bullheads generally are caught on bait, but they will strike artificial flies that simulate baitfish. On the Susquehanna River in Pennsylvania, catfish also rise to the surface to feed on abundant fly hatches at night.

CHAR Brook trout and lake trout actually are chars, closely related to trout but with a different mouth structure. The other two North American members of the char group are the Dolly Varden and the arctic char. Beautiful fish with light spots on a dark skin (trout have dark spots on lighter skin), char readily take flies simulating baitfish, shrimp, and insects.

GRAYLING Strong fighters with long, flowing fins on their backs, both the American and European grayling rise to dry flies. The American grayling typically is a slower biter than its European counterpart,

Arctic grayling

which darts to the surface to take food and artificial flies. Though an American grayling will experiment, striking an unusual fly with its small, papery mouth, the fish often shies from a heavy leader. American grayling group together in schools in lakes and streams in Canada's Northwest Territories and Alaska, as well as in Michigan and some western states,

LITTLE TUNNY   Also improperly called false albacore and bonito, this member of the mackerel family is an extraordinary gamefish for the inshore fly fisher. Often found in the company of bonito, the little tunny of the Atlantic and the Mediterranean grows to more than fifteen pounds of what appears to be solid muscle when it runs from you.

MACKEREL   Built more streamlined than bullets, these iridescent fish hit shiny streamers retrieved very quickly. Exciting fish to catch on light rods, mackerel also are excellent to eat within twenty-four hours of being killed.

MUSKELLUNGE   The largest member of the pike family, a muskie can grow to fifty or sixty pounds. Its strike is savage when a streamer appears to be worth the effort; the fly must look like a large meal, and you should retrieve it quickly, working it all the way to your rod tip, where the fish may strike. A shock tippet is necessary to withstand the muskie's sharp teeth.

PERCH Though they usually offer a sluggish fight, white perch and yellow perch probably are the most delicious freshwater fish, and a sea-run white perch tastes even better. (White perch are more closely related to bass than to yellow perch.) On ponds, perch take a variety of flies including small streamers and nymphs fished slowly, and during a major caddis or mayfly hatch, the fish will feed on the surface. Sea-run white perch hit flies resembling grass shrimp and baitfish, as well as many patterns designed for American shad.

PERMIT AND OTHER JACKS Of the twenty-one species of jacks in American waters, fly fishers regard the permit with the most enthusiasm. It is the most difficult to catch of the three fish that make an angler's "grand slam:" a tarpon, bonefish, and permit in one day. Though fifty-pounders have been recorded, smaller fish are more common in shallow water where fly fishers pursue them. Spooky and apparently myopic, permit take flies resembling small crabs. To catch and release a permit is a rare accomplishment. Many other members of the jack family, including crevalles and horse-eye jacks, also offer fine sport for inshore fly fishers who enjoy fighting fish that always seem to have another run in them.

PICKEREL Among the smallest members of the pike family, pickerel compensate for their size in savagery. Motionless, they lie in the shade and dart out to strike streamers and poppers that appear to be quickly fleeing. Fly-rod bugs simulating frogs, mice, and other floating creatures often are most effective when you drop one within a few feet

Northern Pike

of the fish and let it lie motionless for what seems like forever. When you inch the bug away and the pickerel hits it, the strike is explosive.

PIKE Ferocious predator of arctic waters around the world, the pike is an exceptional adversary for the fly fisher. The fish has powerful jaws in its duckbill mouth, filled with sharp teeth. Though a pike can grow to over fifty pounds, eight- to ten-pound fish are more common. In the spring, a pike charges at long flies that simulate another fish invading its territory. The flaky flesh of a pike tastes delicious except when it comes from very warm water.

RED DRUM   More commonly known as redfish or channel bass, red drum have become popular fly-rod targets along the southern Atlantic and Gulf coasts where thirty- and forty-pounders take brightly colored attractor flies that work equally well on seatrout. Fly fishing for redfish is a sight-hunting game. The fish often are spooky and difficult to approach, making them one of the few gamefish requiring long casts.

LANDLOCKED SALMON   In Maine, fly tiers created such famous streamers as the Grey Ghost and the Black Ghost specifically for landlocked salmon, but the inland version of the Atlantic salmon also strikes tiny insect imitations. As soon as the winter ice melts in northern New England, many anglers celebrate the arrival of spring by trolling flies with tandem hooks for landlocked salmon.

In the western states, the kokanee salmon is the dwarf, landlocked version of the sockeye. In Japan, where the fish also lives, anglers call it *Benimasa*. Fish managers have introduced the kokanee to waters in several eastern states, where the fish strike trolled streamers.

PACIFIC SALMON   Five species of Pacific salmon thrive in North America, and all are exciting to catch on a fly rod. The sixth species, cherry salmon, is native to Asia. Sockeye, pink, and chum salmon are great gamefish, but Chinook and coho salmon are the fly fisher's favorite targets. The Chinook, or "king" salmon, is the largest Pacific salmon, growing to over 100 pounds. The coho, or "silver," is a spectacular leaper when hooked. In inshore waters such as Puget Sound (where resident Chinook are called "blackmouths"), Chinook and coho strike large streamers resembling herring. When they enter their spawning streams, Pacific salmon stop eating, but still, they strike flies and other lures. Unlike Atlantic salmon, which return to the sea after spawning, Pacific salmon spawn once and die.

SHAD   Commonly referred to as "the poor angler's salmon" because of their spectacular leaping ability and mint-bright flanks, American shad are common from Florida to New England, and in many western coastal rivers where they have been introduced. Each spring, shad migrate from the salt water to their native streams where they strike brightly colored flies drifted on the stream bottom. Though bony, American shad are delicious to eat. The smaller hickory shad is not nearly as delectable, although some fishers enjoy it smoked. The hickory is an extraordinary jumper and fighter when hooked.

SNOOK   The common snook, or *robalo*, is native to coastal waters from Florida and the Gulf coast to Brazil, where it strikes flies cast among mangrove roots, fallen tangles, jetties, and other obstructions in tidal creeks. Rarely finicky about which fly patterns to attack, snook jump and run when hooked. Strong fish, they often head for oyster bars and dense roots, which easily snap fly leaders. The black snook, or *robalo prieto*, has similar habits, but it inhabits Pacific estuaries from Baja California to Peru.

SPOTTED SEATROUT A cousin of the weakfish, spotted seatrout are especially popular among fly fishers in Florida and throughout the Gulf of Mexico. They cast small streamer flies and poppers to attract fish feeding on shrimp and small baitfish near shore. White-and-red, yellow-and-red, and orange flies seem to be the most attractive to spotted seatrout. Delicious to eat, the fish ought to be iced as soon as it is killed.

STEELHEAD Steelhead look like giant rainbow trout and often act like submarine-launched missiles. Natives of North America's west coast, they are similar to salmon: Born in freshwater streams, they migrate to sea and return to spawn. Unlike Pacific salmon, however, steelhead do not die after spawning. Steelhead take a variety of wet flies, many of which look like salmon patterns, as well as artificial eggs and sometimes dry flies. Like Pacific salmon, steelhead have been transplanted to the Great Lakes, where they thrive and provide exceptional fly fishing action.

STRIPED BASS Artificially introduced into freshwater impoundments and West Coast estuaries, stripers are fine gamefish wherever you find them. Stripers migrate along the Atlantic coast from Canada to northern Florida, but they are most abundant along New England and the middle Atlantic states. Some anglers refer to stripers as rockfish, because of their fondness for hugging rocky shorelines and reefs. Fly fishers most often cast baitfish imitations to stripers, but the fish also take poppers, worm simulations, and floating bugs that look like miniature crabs. Because stripers commonly feed at night, the best times to catch them on a fly are just after sunset and before dawn.

SUNFISH The most colorful fish in fresh waters, bluegills, bream, pumpkinseeds, and the other sunfish are fun to catch on a fly rod. Voracious eaters, sunfish strike a variety of flies including most nymphs, dry flies, small streamers, and poppers. Because sunfish have small mouths, flies should have hooks smaller than #8. In addition to offering a lot of

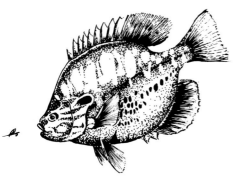

Sunfish

Tarpon

fun, sunfish provide good fishing practice, and they are very tasty.

TARPON The silver king can weigh over 200 pounds and is strong enough to tow a boat for miles. Tarpon range from Cape Hatteras to Brazil in the Americas, and along the equatorial coast of West Africa, where anglers have taken fish of over 250 pounds apiece on conventional tackle. Simply hooking a giant tarpon is the dream of many experienced fly fishers. And landing a tail-walking silver king on a fly is a bonus. "Baby" tarpon in the twenty-pound category hit drab streamers as well as the brightly colored feathers that many anglers cast for larger tarpon.

TROUT More than two dozen kinds of trout and char swim in American waters, and all of them strike artificial flies, representing a wide variety of natural foods, from minuscule midges to mice. But fly fishermen don't love trout because of the fish's willingness to take flies—sometimes, trout seem downright unwilling to take *anything*.

Trout anglers love the *places* trout love: clear, cold waters, far from crowds. With few exceptions, trout cannot—or will not—live in cities. Any city that does have a stream where trout can live comfortably is probably a good place for people, too.

As you grow into fly fishing, you will discover that more has been written about trout than any other gamefish. If you're an empiricist, you can devote a lifetime to studying trout biology and behavior. If you're a romanticist, you will love the stories of spring creeks, mountain streams, and trout sipping flies from the surface.

Weakfish

WEAKFISH The only weak part of a weakfish is its papery mouth, which tears easily. Also called squeteague, the weakfish is a strong fighter that strikes flies simulating grass shrimp and small baitfish. Because of its soft mouth, you should use a net to land the weakfish—otherwise the hook may tear free. The fish tastes delicious when you cook it soon after it is killed.

WHITEFISH Some trout-fishing purists regard lake whitefish and mountain whitefish as "trash" fish, probably because the fish are less discriminating about the flies they take. That very quality, however, makes them fun to catch, and the mountain whitefish of western streams provide action throughout the winter, taking a variety of small flies. The flesh of both lake and mountain whitefish is tasty, and the liver of the lake whitefish makes an excellent pâté.

OFFSHORE BIG GAME Billfish, sharks, and tuna all strike flies. So do wahoo, king mackerel, and other speedsters found offshore. Trolling hookless lures, anglers "tease" the fish into casting range. Then, one angler pulls the hookless lure away from the fish, and the fly fisher presents his fly to the attacking fish. Chumming for sharks and tuna also works: The angler throws chopped bait into the water to attract feeding fish and then casts a fly to them.

INSHORE PANFISH Inshore fly fishing is not limited to "glamorous" gamefish such as tarpon, bonefish, and stripers. Sea robins, flounder, and even skates and rays hit flies. Small sea perch, snappers, and other tasty panfish are abundant and fun to catch on light fly tackle. Many inshore species of panfish are found close to rocky shores, docks, and bridges—within range of a short cast.

10

COMMON SENSE AND SAFETY

“Nothing is so disturbing to the joys of trout fishing as to step on a slippery rock while wading a stream and go hip boots over tincups. There are several ways of avoiding this. Some people wear nonskid chain devices attached to their boots. Some people wear stocking-foot waders and hobnailed or felt-soled shoes. Some people with more gray matter just stay the hell out of trout streams.**”**

—ED ZERN
To Hell with Fishing

Always wear glasses when you are fishing. Polarized sunglasses will help you see fish as they protect your eyes from the harmful ultraviolet rays of the sun.

To protect your eyes from getting scratched as you walk through the woods and from getting hooked while you're casting, wear sunglasses—even on cloudy days—and clear safety glasses for night fishing.

If someone does get hooked in an eye, do not try to remove the hook. Cut the leader off, bandage *both* eyes to keep them closed, and find a physician immediately.

Here are more thoughts on safety and common sense:

• Removing a hook from someone's skin is easy if the hook is barbless; usually, you can back it out.

• There are two ways to remove a barbed hook from someone's skin, but neither is pleasant—another reason for squeezing down hook barbs before you start fishing.

The first thing to do when someone is hooked is to cut the leader next to the fly.

Sometimes, you may have to push the point through and outside the skin again so the barb is exposed. Push it through quickly and with enough force so you don't have to try again. With wire cutters, clip the hook near the bend and remove both ends.

Here's another way to remove a barbed hook:

Make a loop of heavy leader material or fly line, twelve to fifteen inches in diameter.

Wrap the loop around your hand so you have a good, strong grip on it.

Wrap the other end of the loop inside the bend of the hook, but do not put any pressure on the hook with the loop—that would hurt.

With your free hand, press the eye of the hook down against your companion's skin and get ready to pull the hook back and out with the loop: Yank it out fast and with plenty of force so that it comes out on the first try. Your companion is not going to give you a second chance.

Then apply some antiseptic ointment from your first-aid kit.

• Wear a hat to prevent your head from getting hooked and sunburned.

• Use a sunscreen to prevent skin cancer.

• Wade wisely. Fish usually are closer than you think; if you cast from the bank, you probably will catch as many or more fish than you will by wading across a stream. If you must wade into flowing water, shuffle *into* the current sideways so the water has less surface to push against.

• When you're fishing with a companion, lock arms and wade close together through heavy currents: That's the angler's version of four-wheel drive.

• When you're alone, a wading staff with a metal tip will give you additional support.

• Felt soles and metal cleats will give you more traction on slippery rocks, but they do not guarantee that you will not slip. Wade slowly and cautiously.

Techniques for wading: The buddy system (left), and using a staff on your downstream side (right).

• Do not wear shoes inside your waders.

• Be aware of changes in water levels due to tides or dam releases.

• Wear a belt around the outside of chest waders to prevent water from flooding your boots when you fall in, and invest in a safety collar that inflates to keep your head afloat.

• Keep your vest pockets zipped closed to prevent your fly boxes from floating away when you fall in.

• If you fall in a river, try to position your feet so they are down-current and use your arms to maneuver yourself into shallow water.

• Keep a set of dry clothes in your car.

• In your vest, keep a small first-aid kit and a lightweight rain jacket.

• To be comfortable, wear layers of clothing that you can remove as the day warms.

• When a thunderstorm is approaching, get out of the water and find shelter *away* from tall trees.

• Before you embark on a wilderness fishing trip, be certain your tetanus shot is up to date.

• In snake country, always be sure that you can see what is ahead of you as you climb up a stream bank.

• Carry pliers to remove hooks from bluefish, northern pike, and other fish with sharp teeth.

• On salt water and large lakes, always keep a compass aboard your boat, no matter how small the boat or how familiar the waters. A sudden fog can disorient you quickly.

11

MAKING YOUR OWN FLIES

> **"**Over the years I have labored at my fly-tying
> labors long after the rest of the house is
> asleep, trying to find that one classic fly...Ten
> years ago I developed an interesting little
> nymph that may be the answer. It is made
> from hairs clipped from my chest and I've had
> fair success with it. I shall try a few more of
> these soon, for some of the hair is grey now
> and the new color scheme may make the
> difference between mediocrity and
> brilliance.**"**
>
> **—NELSON BRYANT**
> Fresh Air, Bright Water

You're going to catch some memorable fish with your fly rod,
but none will be as gratifying as the first fish you catch on a fly you
have made yourself.

Like fly fishing, making flies is as simple or as complex as you
want to make it. Fishers who make their own flies are fly tiers (sometimes spelled "tyers") because they build flies by winding and tying
the materials for an artificial fly to a hook.

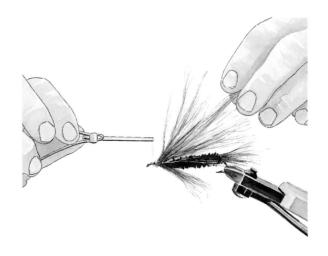

Fly tying is an excellent way to expand the range of your sport.

Fly tying is economical. When you calculate only the cost of materials and tools, a fly you tie costs less than ten percent of a fly you would buy. Labor accounts for much of the price.

If you like to work with your hands, you probably will find fly tying to be like fly fishing—relaxing and stimulating. You may even find tying flies to be as satisfying as fishing them, particularly when you design your own flies.

To start tying your own flies, you will need some basic tools:

FLY VISE to hold the hook in place while you attach materials to it.

SMALL PAIR OF NEEDLE-NOSE PLIERS to squeeze down hook barbs to make the hook penetrate effectively when a fish strikes, and to make it easier to remove later. For small hooks, the jaws of your vise also will work to squeeze down barbs.

HOOK SHARPENER hones the point of a hook to needle sharpness. To test a hook point, gently rub it against your thumbnail; the point is sharp enough when it sticks.

BOBBIN to hold your thread and to help you wind it precisely.

BOBBIN THREADER simply is a loop of fine, stiff wire that makes it easy to thread a bobbin. Stick the wire down the narrow neck of your bobbin so it protrudes from the bottom, near the thread. Run the end of the thread through the bottom loop, then pull the loop and the thread up through the tube. The bobbin threader also works as a simple **WHIP FINISHING TOOL** to make the head of a fly.

SCISSORS   with fine tips to clip and trim all of the various materials you will use.

HACKLE PLIERS   grip the feathers, or "hackles," that go into a fly.

BODKIN AND HALF-HITCH TOOL   The bodkin is the needle used to apply cement, to rough up fly bodies so they look buggy, and for a variety of other jobs. On the opposite end, the half-hitch tool makes it easy to tie a half-hitch knot.

HEAD CEMENT OR LAQUER   to seal the final knot so it won't unravel. **CLEAR ENAMEL FINGERNAIL POLISH** is a fine substitute for lacquer.

Generally, fly tiers follow a "recipe" to build a particular fly pattern. The recipe lists all the materials you will need, and usually the order in which they go on the hook.

The Woolly Worm is one of the most effective freshwater flies ever created and one of the easiest to make. Here's the recipe for the pattern:

WOOLY WORM
Hook: #12–2, 2XL
Thread: Black
Tail: Red wool yarn
Hackle: Grizzly, palmered
Body: Medium black chenille

Some fly recipes call for a specific hook design and even recommend a particular hook manufacturer. This recipe lets you select the size you want, from a small #12 to a large #2. The designation 2XL means that the hook shank should be two sizes longer than a standard hook. The code 1XL would mean one size longer than a standard length; XS would mean "extra short." The drawing of a fly hook illustrates its parts.

The thread is standard fly-tying thread, waxed, so it grips materials securely. Fly-tying thread comes in various sizes and colors for various patterns. Black is the standard color, but feel free to use another color.

The tail material for a Woolly Worm is wool knitting yarn, available from fly-fishing outfitters or knitting shops. The standard Woolly Worm pattern specifies red, but some fly tiers prefer fluorescent pink, lime, or yellow. Use any color you like.

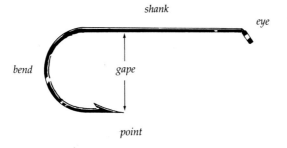

shank

eye

bend

gape

point

Parts of a hook.

"Hackle" is the fly tier's term for chicken feathers wound around the hook so the fibers stick out like ultrafine flower petals. Grizzly is one of many hackle colors: it has alternating bars of black and white. Feel free to use another color. "Palmered" tells you to wind the hackle along the entire length of the fly, from back to front.

Chenille is a spun material traditionally used in sweaters and bedspreads. In fly-fishing stores and knitting shops, chenille is available in various thicknesses, from very thin for small flies to very thick for large flies. Black, brown, and olive probably are the most popular colors for Woolly Worms, but you may use any color that appeals to you.

By tying a half dozen Woolly Worms, you will learn essential skills you can apply to tying other styles of flies. The Woolly Worm simulates stonefly larvae, damselfly nymphs, and other insects that fish eat. By changing the size of the hook and altering the pattern slightly, you can tie a Woolly Bugger, which looks like a leech or possibly a nightcrawler.

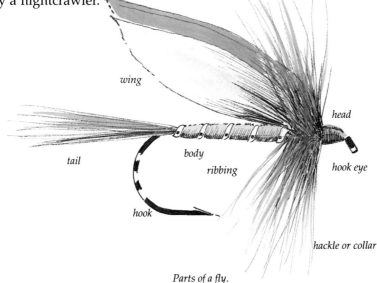

wing

head

tail

body

ribbing

hook eye

hook

hackle or collar

Parts of a fly.

When you're tying a fly, start at the back of the hook, where it bends, and work forward, always anticipating the next material and movement.

By now, you have read the directions that came with your vise, bobbin, and other tools; everything is set up, and the materials to tie a Woolly Worm are at hand. Now open this book so it lies flat next to the vise.

Here are the steps for a right-handed tier; if you are left-handed, please reverse them:

1. Prepare your materials: Cut a piece of wool yarn about the length of the hook. Select a long hackle feather. Cut a piece of chenille, about six inches long and squeeze one end of it between the edge of your thumbnail and your index finger. Scratch away about a half inch of the fuzzy stuff so you can see the thread beneath at the core.

2. To make tying easy, start with a large hook, a #4. Squeeze down the hook barb with the jaws of your vise or your needle-nose pliers.

3. Sharpen the hook point so it sticks when you rub it against the surface of your thumbnail.

4. Insert the hook in the vise, according to the vise-maker's instructions. The head of the vise and the eye of the hook should be pointing to your right. So you don't stick yourself or break the thread later, it's a good idea to hide the hook point in the vise jaws if you can.

5. Hold the bobbin in your right hand, and with your left hand, pull at least six inches of thread from the bobbin's neck. With your right hand an inch or two above the hook and your left hand below the hook, push the thread against the middle of the hook shank.

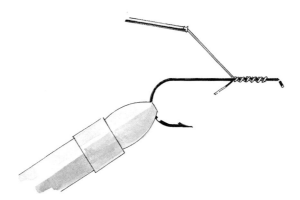

Starting the thread: Wrap the thread toward the bend of the hook. Wind the thread to the hook bend and stop.

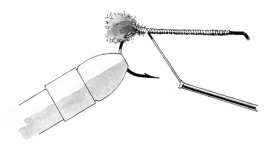

Tying on the tail: Wrap the thread around the hook and the yarn again and again—first toward the eye, then back to the tie-in point at the bend.

Don't move your left hand. With the bobbin in your right hand, wrap the thread around the hook, always in a clockwise motion away from you. Wrap the thread toward the bend of the hook so the thread from the bobbin anchors the thread from your left hand against the hook shank.

Wind the thread to the hook bend and stop.

6. Let the bobbin hang on an inch or two of thread beneath the hook shank, and pick up your scissors with your right hand. Hold the loose thread in your left hand tight above the hook. With the scissors, snip it off close to the hook.

7. With your left thumb and index finger, hold the piece of wool along the top of the hook, with about a quarter inch of yarn sticking out beyond the hook bend. Take the hanging bobbin in your right hand. Lift it directly above the fingers pinching the wool yarn, and as you lift the bobbin, work the thread between the pinched fingers. Now anchor the wool yarn against the top of the hook by bringing the bobbin down on the opposite side of the hook —away from your chest—and bring the thread down through the pinched fingers.

Bring the bobbin beneath the hook and up toward you. Guide the thread up through the pinch again, over the hook, and down through the pinch on the opposite side of the hook. The yarn should be anchored now, so you can release your left-hand pinch. Wrap the thread around the hook and the yarn again and again, first wrapping toward the eye, and then back to the tie-in point at the bend, so the yarn is lashed down securely.

You may once again let the bobbin hang on an inch or two of thread beneath the hook.

If the yarn was too long and some of it is sticking out over the hook eye, trim off the excess yarn just to the left of the eye. A yarn tail, about a quarter inch long, should be sticking out beyond the back of the hook.

Tying on hackle: The wide stem of the feather should extend behind the hook, where it will be out of the way for now.

8. At the hook's bend—the tie-in spot—attach the hackle feather just as you started the yarn: Pinch the narrow tip of the feather between your left thumb and forefinger and hold it against the top of the hook. Take the hanging bobbin in your right hand. Lift it directly above the fingers pinching the hackle tip, and as you lift the bobbin, work the thread between the pinched fingers. Anchor the hackle tip against the top of the hook by bringing the bobbin down through the pinch on the opposite side of the hook—away from your chest.

Bring the bobbin beneath the hook and up toward you. Guide the thread through the pinch again, over the hook, and down through the pinch on the opposite side of the hook. The feather should be anchored now, so you can release your left-hand pinch. Make three more thread wraps around the tie-in point to secure the hackle tip. The wide stem of the feather should extend behind the hook, where it will be out of the way for now.

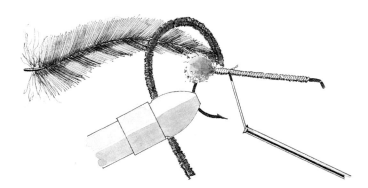

Tying on body material: After tying in the material (in this case chenille) wind forward, directly over the tying thread.

9. It's time to tie in the chenille body. At the tie-in point near the hook bend, use the pinch technique for anchoring the stripped chenille core to the hook. Tightly wrap the thread over the stripped chenille so it stays anchored.

10. In your left hand, hold the hackle and the long piece of chenille behind the hook and out of the way. With the bobbin in your right hand, cover the hook with thread as you wind the thread in clockwise spirals. Wrap toward the eye and stop just behind it.

You may let the bobbin hang on an inch or two of thread beneath the hook.

11. Take the chenille in your right hand and cover the hook with it, wrapping away from your chest, toward the hook eye. Use your left thumbnail and index finger to keep each new wrap tight against the previous one.

Wrap the chenille to just behind the eye, but don't crowd the eye because you still have to make a head.

Wrapping the body: Wrap the chenille to just behind the eye, but don't crowd the eye—you still have to make a head.

Hold the remaining chenille straight above the hook. With your left hand, take the bobbin and make two wraps of thread over the hook, anchoring the chenille as you do so. (At first, this may seem impossible; to wrap the thread over the hook and chenille, guide the bobbin over the hook to the opposite side, and drop it so the thread tightens itself on the chenille.)

With the bobbin in your right hand now, secure the chenille with two more tight wraps of thread.

You may let the bobbin hang beneath the hook as you use your scissors to trim the excess chenille close to the hook shank.

12. Use your half-hitch tool to tie two half-hitch knots over the trimmed chenille:

Hold the tool in your right hand just beneath the fly, with the hole on the end of the tool pointing to the left. Hold the bobbin in your left hand.

Bring the bobbin toward you, under the half-hitch tool. Keep the thread tight and make one complete wrap around the tool so the bobbin is beneath the half-hitch tool again.

Bring the hole of the half-hitch tool to the eye of the hook. With the bobbin in your left hand, slide the thread loop off the tool and onto the hook. Tighten the thread, and you have tied a half hitch.

Now tie a second half-hitch to lock in the first.

13. With your right hand, grasp the end of hackle feather, and wind it forward—this is called "palmering"—like the stripes of a candy cane, toward the eye of the hook. When you reach the eye, don't crowd it with the hackle because you still must make a head.

Hold the end of the feather straight above the hook with your right hand.

With your left hand, take the bobbin and make two wraps over the hook, dropping the bobbin on the opposite side as you did before.

With the feather anchored in place, switch the bobbin to your right hand and make two or three more thread wraps to secure the feather tightly.

You may let the bobbin hang beneath the hook as you trim away the excess feather.

14. With the half-hitch tool, tie two half-hitch knots. (If you were tying a minuscule midge, the fly would be finished now, but because the Woolly Worm is so much larger, there are two more steps.)

15. Whip-finish the Woolly Worm with your bobbin threader. With left thumb and index finger, hold the fine wire loop on top of the fly with a little bit of the loop extending out beyond the hook eye.

With the bobbin in your right hand, make six to eight wraps—firm but not tight—around the hook and the wire loop.

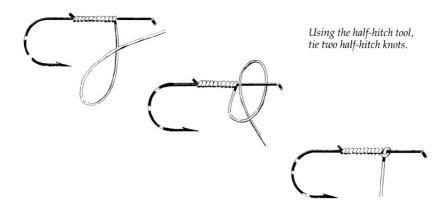

Using the half-hitch tool, tie two half-hitch knots.

Palmering: With your right hand, grasp the end of the hackle feather and wind it forward—like the stripes of a candy cane—toward the eye of the hook.

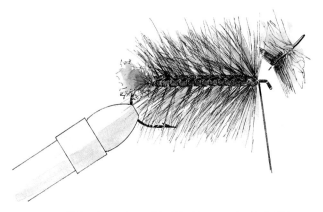

Trimming palmered hackle: You may let the bobbin hang beneath the hook as you trim away excess feather.

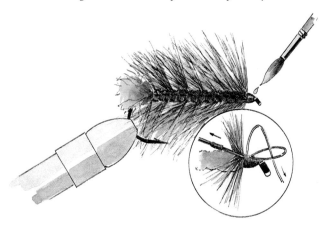

Whip finish the head with your bobbin threader, then add head cement or lacquer carefully.

A Woolly Bugger completed: This will catch freshwater fish almost anywhere in the world !

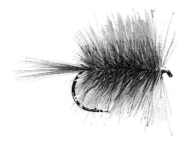

Three flies tied with similar methodology: Marabou Streamer (top), Woolly Bugger (middle), and Bivisible (bottom).

Pull about four inches of thread from the bobbin with your right hand. With your left thumb and index finger, pinch the newly formed head and the wire loop beneath it.

Clip the thread near the top of the bobbin, and place the end of the thread through the wire loop.

Still pinching the head with your left hand, use your right hand to grasp the other end of the bobbin threader and pull it back so it slides beneath the thread wraps and brings the end of the thread with it.

16. Snip off the excess thread and coat the head with two applications of head cement or enamel fingernail polish.

Congratulations. You have just tied a fly that will probably catch freshwater fish anywhere in the world.

You also have learned fundamental skills that you may apply to tying other patterns. To develop your tying skills and stock your fly box, tie a dozen or more Woolly Worms in various sizes and colors, then go on to other patterns.

Instead of using a short piece of yarn for the tail, use a clump of soft marabou feather the same length as the hook shank to create a Woolly Bugger, another all-purpose fly.

To make an effective baitfish imitation, tie the Woolly Worm on a very long hook with a silver or white chenille body and add a long, white wing of marabou or another soft material.

On a tiny hook, the basic Woolly Worm design with a short elk-hair wing looks like a caddisfly.

Experiment with materials and tying techniques. Relax and release your mind from day-to-day stress. When you're tying flies on a cold winter's night, you're bound to hook some trophy fish in the pools of your mind.

RECOMMENDED FLIES

Selecting the best fly for a particular fishing situation is easy when you take the time to observe the water and collect some insect samples.

Match the fish's natural food with an artificial that is the same size, shape, and color, and fish it so it behaves like a living creature. If you find a lot of tiny olive-colored bugs with upright wings floating on the surface, for example, tie on a tiny olive-colored artificial fly with upright wings. Then cast the fly so it drifts along at the same speed as the real flies around it.

When the water's surface holds no insects but fish are feeding on top, use an insect net to see if mayflies or caddisflies are emerging just beneath the surface.

When you cannot see insects or fish, look on the bottom for insect nymphs and larvae, or watch for baitfish and crustaceans. The following recommendations are basic shopping lists for the fly patterns you may need. The correct fly size varies from one body of water to the next, and sometimes from pool to pool. It's wise to buy at least three sizes of each fly pattern. And buy three flies in each size.

When you're traveling to an unfamiliar area, however, ask your guide or outfitter which flies to bring, or visit a fly shop at your destination to buy the best patterns for current conditions.

Here are some suggested fly patterns for you to buy or tie:

ALL-PURPOSE TROUT FLIES

Adams	Woolly Worm	Beetles, assorted colors
Royal Wulff, Gray	Woolly Bugger	and sizes
Wulff, White Wulff	Humpy	Cricket
Elkhair Caddis, various	Black and Cinnamon Ants	Grasshopper
colors and sizes	Griffith's Gnat	Gold-Ribbed Hare's
Sparkle Caddis Pupa,	Muddler Minnow	Ear Nymph
various colors	White Marabou Streamer	Pheasant Tail Nymph
and sizes		

ADDITIONAL TROUT FLIES FOR THE NORTHEAST

Hendrickson	Slate Drake	Black Caddis
Light Cahill	Blue-Winged Olive	Gray Ghost Streamer
Quill Gordon	Black Gnat	Mickey Finn Streamer
Black Quill	Green Caddis	Black Ghost Streamer
Pale Evening Dun		

ADDITIONAL TROUT FLIES FOR THE SOUTHERN APPALACHIANS

Red Quill
Irresistible
Quill Gordon
Ginger Quill
March Brown
Black Gnat

Gray Fox Variant
Light Cahill
Blue-Winged Olive
My Pet (A regional nymph
    pattern available in most
    southern fly shops)

Tellico Nymph
Black Nose Dace Streamer
Gray Ghost Streamer

ADDITIONAL TROUT FLIES FOR THE MIDWEST

Michigan Caddis
    (to imitate the giant
    Hexagenia limbata
    mayfly)
Yellow Drake
Hendrickson

Red Quill
Blue-Winged Olive
Pale Evening Dun
Trico
March Brown Nymph
Zug Bug

Roe Bug,
    various colors
Olive Matuka Streamer
Black and Yellow
    Marabou Streamer

ADDITIONAL TROUT FLIES FOR THE ROCKIES

Large Stonefly patterns,
    such as the Sofa Pillow
    or Salmon Fly
Gray Drake
Pale Morning Dun
Blue Dun

March Brown
Blue-Winged Olive
Light Cahill
Trico
Dark Stonefly
    Nymphs

Montana Nymphs
White Zonker Streamer
Black Zonker Streamer
Marabou Muddler Streamer
San Juan Worm

ADDITIONAL TROUT FLIES FOR THE WEST

Pale Morning Dun
Green Drake
Gray Drake
Blue-Winged Olive

March Brown
Light Cahill
Blue Dun
Great Western Lead-Wing

Black Gnat
Muskrat Nymph
Damselfly Nymph
Carey Special

ALL-PURPOSE BASS FLIES

Cork, foam, and
    deer-hair
    poppers
Dahlberg Diver
Slider

Rabbit-Strip Leeches
    and Snakes
Clouser's Crayfish and
    similar patterns
Clouser's Minnow

Nix's Sunfish Flies
Bucktail streamers, various
    colors and sizes
White or Black Zonkers

ALL-PURPOSE SALTWATER FLIES

Lefty's Deceiver, various colors
    and sizes
Brooks Blonde, various colors
    and sizes

Bucktail streamers, various colors and sizes
Crazy Charlie (for bonefish)
    various colors and sizes
Shrimp flies

RECOMMENDED READING

BOOKS TO HELP YOU INCREASE YOUR FISHING SKILLS:
• •

BORGER, GARY A. *Naturals, A Guide to Food Organisms of the Trout*. Stackpole Books, 1980. A thorough key to identifying and simulating aquatic insects and the other things trout eat.

CAUCCI, AL AND BOB NASTASI. *Hatches II*. Lyons & Burford, Publishers, 1990. A truly complete guide to fishing the hatches of North American trout streams.

COMBS, TREY. *Steelhead Fly Fishing*. Lyons & Burford, Publishers, 1991. A beautiful book containing everything you need to know about steelhead fishing.

HARVEY, GEORGE W. *Techniques of Trout Fishing and Fly Tying*. Revised and augmented edition, Lyons & Burford, Publishers, 1990. The author's advice about leaders is invaluable.

HUMPHREYS, JOE. *Joe Humphreys's Trout Tactics, Updated and Expanded*. Stackpole Books, 1993. A treasury of tactics and tips to help you hook more trout. The chapter on water temperature is especially important.

JAWOROWSKI, ED. *The Cast*. Stackpole Books, 1991. Once you feel comfortable with a fly rod, the author advises you to forget what you have learned here.

KREH, LEFTY. *Longer Fly Casting*. Lyons & Burford, Publishers, 1991. A compact handbook to help you lengthen your casts and correct problems.

LAFONTAINE, GARY. *The Dry Fly, New Angles*. Greycliff Publishing, 1990. Learn nothing more than the Ten Commandments of Stealth, and you will be a more effective angler—but there is much, much more unconventional advice to learn here.

MERWIN, JOHN (editor). *Stillwater Trout*. Nick Lyons Books/Lyons & Burford, Publishers, 1980. Experts from all over the United States and Great Britain offer advice on fishing lakes and ponds.

MURRAY, HARRY. *Fly Fishing for Smallmouth Bass*. Nick Lyons Books/Lyons & Burford, Publishers, 1989. A handbook of tactics, techniques, and flies for catching streamborn smallmouths.

ROSENBAUER, TOM. *Reading Trout Streams*. Nick Lyons Books/Lyons & Burford, Publishers, 1988. A detailed guide with fine photographs to help you find trout on unfamiliar streams.

SWISHER, DOUG and CARL RICHARDS. *Emergers*. Lyons & Burford, Publishers, 1991. An exploration of stream insects when they are most vulnerable to trout.

TABORY, LOU. *Inshore Fly Fishing*. Lyons & Burford, Publishers, 1992. The best information source for northeastern saltwater fly fishers, the book also contains advice applicable to the Pacific Northwest and the western Gulf coast.

BOOKS TO HELP YOU INCREASE YOUR FLY-TYING SKILLS:

GARTSIDE, JACK. *Fly Patterns for The Adventurous Tyer* and *Flies for The 21st Century*. Self-published by Jack Gartside, 10 Sachem St., Boston, Mass. 02120.

FLICK, ART (editor). *Art Flick's Master Fly-Tying Guide*. Crown Publishers, 1972. Some of America's best tiers explain their techniques.

KAUFMANN, RANDALL. *American Nymph Fly Tying Manual*. Frank Amato Publications, 1975. A collection of techniques and patterns for all the nymphs you'll need including several Pacific Northwest patterns that catch fish anywhere.

LEISER, ERIC. *The Book of Fly Patterns*. Alfred A. Knopf, 1987. More than 1,000 modern fly patterns will fill all your needs for trout, salmon, and saltwater fish.

LEONARD, J. EDSON. *Flies*. (1950) Most recent edition published by Lyons & Burford, Publishers. Containing 2,200 patterns, *Flies* is a classic.

SHAW, HELEN. *Fly Tying*. (1983) Most recent edition published by Lyons & Burford, Publishers. Easy-to-follow photographs guide you through fundamental fly-tying techniques—from your side of the vise.

TALLEUR, DICK. *The Versatile Fly Tyer*. Nick Lyons Books/Lyons & Burford, Publishers, 1990. The author makes difficult patterns easy to tie with Dick's Tricks and step-by-step instructions.

RECOMMENDED GENERAL-REFERENCE BOOKS

MC CLANE, A.J. (editor). *McClane's New Standard Fishing Encyclopedia and International Angling Guide*. Henry Holt and Company, 1974. From aawa to zooplankton, the encyclopedia is a complete source of fishing information.

SCHULLERY, PAUL. *American Fly Fishing, A History*. Lyons & Burford, Publishers, 1987. From Europe in the 1200s to twentieth-century America, the author traces the history and development of fly fishing.

SOSIN, MARK and JOHN CLARK. *Through the Fish's Eye*. Harper & Row, Publishers, 1973. An interesting general guide to why fish behave as they do.

SOUCIE, GARY. *Soucie's Fishing Data Book*. Nick Lyons Books/Lyons & Burford, Publishers, 1985. A collection of statistics and charts on everything from preferred water temperatures for spawning fish to cholesterol counts and vitamins contained in edible fish.

BOOKS TO MAKE YOU LOVE FLY FISHING EVEN MORE:
● ●

CHATHAM, RUSSELL (editor). *Silent Seasons*. E. P. Dutton, 1978. Twenty-seven stories by seven American experts on fishing, swapping, and other essential elements in the angler's life.

GAMMON, CLIVE. *I Know a Good Place*. David R. Godine, Publisher, 1989. From Nantucket to the Falkland Islands, travel the fishing world with these stories from *Sports Illustrated*.

HUGHES, DAVE. *An Angler's Astoria*. Frank Amato Publications, 1982. A collection of timeless stories and essays about fishing in the Pacific Northwest.

HUMPHREY, WILLIAM. *Open Season*. Delacorte Press/Seymour Lawrence, 1986. Besides *My Moby Dick* and *The Spawning Run*, the author's most celebrated fishing novellas, this collection contains eleven other stories about the outdoors.

LYONS, NICK. *Spring Creek*. The Atlantic Monthly Press, 1992. Learn and laugh with the author as he shares a stream, his sport, and his soul.

LYONS, NICK (editor). *Fisherman's Bounty*. (1970) A Fireside Book, published by Simon & Schuster, 1988. A treasury of the world's best stories about fishing and fishermen.

RAYMOND, STEVE. *The Year of the Angler*. Winchester Press, 1983. Explore the seasons of a modern thinker who fishes in the Pacific Northwest.

TAPPLY, WILLIAM G., *Opening Day and Other Neuroses*. Nick Lyons Books/Lyons & Burford, Publishers, 1990. Wandering waters and the mind of an addicted angler.

TRAVER, ROBERT. *Trout Madness*. (1960) A Fireside Book, published by Simon & Schuster, 1989. "A Dissertation on the Symptoms and Pathology of This Incurable Disease by One of its Victims."

TRAVER, ROBERT. *Trout Magic*. (1974) A Fireside Book, published by Simon & Schuster, 1989. More madness, mirth, and mermaids.

A GLOSSARY OF COMMON FLY-FISHING TERMS

ACTION A term to describe the stiffness of a fishing rod as well as where it flexes. A fast-action rod feels stiff except near the top where it flexes; a slow- or parabolic-action rod flexes along much of its length.

AQUATIC INSECT Any one of several flies that hatch from eggs deposited in the water and live beneath the surface during the early stages of life. Fish prey on immature insects beneath the surface and on the adults as they emerge from the water and then return to lay eggs.

ARBOR The core at the center of a fly reel's spool.

ATTRACTOR FLY A fly that stimulates fish to strike even though the fly does not appear to resemble the fish's natural food. Examples include the Royal Coachman dry fly and the Mickey Finn streamer.

BACKING Flexible, braided line that runs between the reel and the fly line. Backing allows a fish to make long runs.

BAITFISH Any of a variety of minnows that are prey to larger fish.

BANK The elevated shoreline on a body of water.

BAR A mound on the bottom of a body of water.

BARB The raised piece of metal immediately behind the point of a hook. The barb makes it difficult for the hook to come loose from a fish's mouth. The barb also impedes the hook from penetrating the fish's mouth when it bites. For more hooking power, eliminate the barb by squeezing it down with a pair of pliers.

BEACHING Subduing a hooked fish by dragging or coaxing it aground.

BELLY The thickest section of a fly line.

BLANK The shaft of a fly rod.

BRACKISH WATER A mixture of fresh water and salt water, often found in coastal marshes.

BUCKTAIL A style of fly, made with hair from a deer's tail, that simulates a baitfish.

BUTT The lower section of a fly rod or the thicker end of a leader, connecting it to the fly line.

CADDISFLIES A group of mothlike aquatic insects that are prey for trout, bass, and panfish.

CHALK STREAM The British term for a highly alkaline, gently flowing body of water comparable to the limestone streams of Pennsylvania.

CHANNEL A depression, usually formed by current, on the bottom of a stream or tidal area.

CHAR A group of fish closely related to trout. The brook trout is a char.

CHUM Natural bait, usually chopped or ground, and thrown into the water to attract fish.

CLEATS Strips of metal on wading-boot soles that bite into ice, algae, and other slippery surfaces to prevent a fisher from falling.

COMPOUND LEADER A nearly invisible connection between the fly line and the fly, made of nylon monofilament sections tied together so the leader tapers from a thick butt to a narrow tip.

COVE An indentation in the shoreline of a large body of water.

CRAYFISH The freshwater version of a lobster that is prey for a variety of game fish.

CREEL The container, often made of straw or fabric, in which anglers keep and carry dead fish.

CRUSTACEANS A group of freshwater and saltwater animals with an external skeleton, such as shrimp, lobsters, and scuds.

CURRENT The flow of water caused by gravity or tidal action.

DAMSELFLY A large aquatic insect often found in ponds, lakes, and the quiet waters of streams. A variety of fish eat damselfly nymphs and adults.

DAPPING A method of fishing for trout that lie tight to a bank. Instead of casting to the fish, the angler sneaks up to the shoreline and extends the rod tip over the water, dangling the fly over the water and dropping it to the surface, slightly upcurrent of the fish, so the fly drifts without drag.

DEAD DRIFT A fishing technique that allows the fly, affected by the current only, to move downstream.

DENSITY A term for comparing the weight of a fly line or leader to the weight of water. High-density lines weigh much more than water, so they sink faster than low-density lines.

DOUBLE-TAPER A fly-line design in which both ends are tapered so that when one end wears out, the angler may reverse the line on the reel.

DOWNSTREAM The direction in which water is flowing.

DRAG (FLY) The unnatural movement of an artificial fly. Usually caused by water currents or wind pushing or pulling the leader, drag causes fish to reject a fly.

DRAG (REEL) The braking mechanism inside a fly reel.

DRAGONFLY A large aquatic insect that looks similar to a damselfly, it most frequently occurs in slow streams or ponds, but several species inhabit gravel bottoms of riffles and rapids. Many species of fish prey on dragonfly nymphs and adults.

DRESSING The materials that make up a fly. Also, a substance that makes a fly or a fly line float.

DRIFT An artificial fly's path as it moves with the current. Drift also describes the downstream movement of a group of insects, crustaceans, or worms.

DRY FLY An artificial fly designed to float on the water's surface.

DUN An adult mayfly before it mates. On the water's surface, duns look like tiny sailboats, usually with dull gray wings.

EDDY A place in a stream, generally in an indentation or behind an obstruction, where the water swirls in the opposite direction of the stream's main current.

EMERGER An aquatic insect at the stage of life when it swims to the water's surface as a nymph or pupa, to become an adult.

FALSE CAST Throwing a fly line backward and forward, always keeping it aloft, to gain distance, to dry a damp fly, or to practice.

FILM The rubbery surface of the water, from which fish take some of their food.

FINGERLING The immature stage of a gamefish when it is about the length of a finger.

FLAT A broad, shallow area in a stream, lake, or tidal water.

FLOTANT A substance that adds buoyancy to flies, leaders, and fly line.

FREESTONE STREAM A body of water that flows over a gravel- or rock-covered bottom. The source usually is runoff from rain, snow, or glaciers.

FRY The first stage in the development of a fish after it hatches from the egg.

GRILSE An adolescent Atlantic salmon.

GUIDES (ROD) The metal loops aligned along the length of a fly rod through which the line passes. The guide closest to the reel is the stripping guide; at the tip of the rod is the tip-top.

HACKLE Feathers, usually from the neck and back of a chicken or game bird, used in making artificial flies.

HANDLE The grip, usually made of cork, for holding a fly rod. Also, the crank on a fly reel used for winding in line.

HATCH The period of time when a large number of aquatic insects emerge from the water. Also, the mass of insects as they emerge.

HAUL A quick but slight tug on the fly line to increase its speed during the pickup, the backcast, or the forward cast.

HOLD The place in a stream where a fish finds relief from the current as it waits to intercept food. A hiding spot usually is nearby.

HOOK EYE The loop at the front of a hook, used to attach the leader.

HOOK KEEPER The small ring or rectangular piece of wire just above a fly rod handle where a fisher keeps a fly.

HOOK SHANK The top—and usually the longest—part of a hook, from the back of the eye to the place where the hook begins to bend.

HOOK SIZE A relative number that indicates the distance from the shank to the point, or the gap. The larger the number, the smaller the hook. Artificial flies generally run from the large #5/0 to the small #28. Added to the number, letters indicate the shank's length; for example, XS is the abbreviation for Extra Short, XL for Extra Long.

INLET The stream feeding a lake, pond, or tidal estuary.

JIGGING The bouncing motion an angler imparts to a weighted fly on the bottom of a body of water.

KNOTLESS LEADER The nearly invisible connection between the fly line and the fly, made from a single strand of tapered nylon.

KORKERS A brand name for a sandal that attaches to wading boots to prevent a fisher from slipping on slick surfaces.

LANDING Capturing a fish.

LARVA The grub-like stage of an aquatic insect such as a caddisfly after it hatches from the egg and before it becomes a pupa. Also, the artificial fly designed to simulate that stage of an insect's life.

LEADER The nearly invisible connection between the fly line and the fly.

LEADER STRAIGHTENER A piece of rubber or leather that removes coils from a leader using the heat generated by friction.

LEADER WALLET A container with envelopes for storing leaders while you are fishing.

LEECH A flattened aquatic worm, commonly called a bloodsucker, or the artificial fly simulating it.

LIMESTONE STREAM A highly alkaline body of water flowing from springs with relatively consistent temperatures throughout the year.

LOOP In fly casting, the candy-cane shape of the line's flight path on the backcast and forward cast. In knot tying, a closed circle at the end of a length of fly line or leader. In fly tying, a U-shaped length of thread used to create a chenille made with cut fur, marabou, or other materials.

LOOP-TO-LOOP A quick connection usually for joining running line to a shooting head or the fly line to the leader.

MARABOU A fluffy feather that undulates in the water, adding action to such flies as Woolly Buggers and many streamers.

MATUKA A baitfish imitation that has long feathers lashed to the top of the hook to simulate the back and tail of a small fish.

MAYFLIES A large group of aquatic insects that are prey for a variety of freshwater fish.

MENDING Flipping the rod tip in a rolling motion to reposition the line on the water and reduce drag on the fly.

MIDGE Any one of a group of minuscule aquatic insects that are prey to an assortment of freshwater fish.

MONOFILAMENT Single-strand nylon fishing line used for spinning reels and fly leaders.

MUDDING The term anglers use to describe the activity of a fish feeding on the bottom and stirring up a cloud of mud.

NYMPH The stage of an aquatic insect's life when it lives in an armored body, between hatching from the egg and shucking the armor as it emerges from the water to become an airborne adult.

OUTLET The stream draining a lake or pond.

PALMING A REEL A technique for slowing a hooked fish as it tries to escape. Press the palm of your reel hand against the outer rim of the spool.

PANFISH A generic name for such freshwater fish as perch and sunfish.

PARR The second stage in the life of trout, salmon, and char, when dark, vertical bars, called parr marks, line their flanks.

PICKUP The first stage of an overhead cast, when the fly line comes off the water to begin a backcast.

POCKET The water behind an obstruction in a stream, where the flow decreases and food for fish accumulates.

POLAROID OR POLARIZED LENSES A type of lens for sunglasses that removes the glare from water so the fisher can see beneath the surface.

POOL A stretch of stream that usually is larger and runs deeper and slower than the water above and below it.

POPPER A fly-rod lure that makes an audible pop as the angler retrieves it to attract bass, bluefish, and other surface-feeding fish.

POUND TEST The strength of a fishing line, determined by how much weight it can support before it breaks.

PRESENTATION The final stage of a cast, when the angler places the fly on the water. Also, the way the fisher maneuvers the fly in the water.

PUMPING A technique for subduing a hooked fish. The angler repeatedly lifts the rod tip to pull the fish closer, then lowers the rod and quickly reels in the line gained.

PUPA The stage in the life of a caddisfly or midge between larva and adult, or an artificial that simulates that stage.

RAPIDS A stretch of stream where the water flows quickly over boulders and smaller rocks.

RIFFLE An extremely shallow stretch of stream where the water flows over gravel or small rocks.

RIP Roily water at the mouth of a tidal river or channel where currents collide.

RISE The moment when a fish comes to the surface to take an insect. Also, the time of day when fish are feeding on the surface; for example, the evening rise.

ROLL CAST A technique for moving the fly line in tight places, using the water's resistance, not a backcast, to load the rod. Anglers also use the technique before the pickup to begin a cast.

RUN The flight of a hooked fish trying to escape. Also, a stretch of stream below a riffle or a small creek.

RUNNING LINE Level fly line or heavy monofilament connected between a shooting head and a reel's backing line. Designed to flow easily through the rod guides so the shooting head flies farther.

SELECTIVE FEEDING Occurs when a certain food source is so abundant that fish key in on it alone, rejecting other foods.

SHOAL A shallow area in a body of water.

SHOCK TIPPET A length of wire or heavy monofilament line, between the fly and leader, that can withstand abrasion from a fish's teeth or bill.

SHOOTING HEAD A short section of fly line designed to cast farther than standard lines.

SINKING TIP A fly line design that allows most of the line to float except the end, which is weighted so it takes the leader and fly beneath the water's surface.

SKATING The action an angler imparts to high-riding flies, such as spiders, by pulling the imitation across the water's surface.

SLACK Line that is free of tension; it impedes casting but assists the drag-free presentation of a fly on the water.

SLIDER A style of bass bug that cuts through the water's surface as the angler retrieves it.

SLOUGH A narrow, slow-flowing channel created by a faster stream changing paths or by human design for irrigation or drainage.

SMOLT The third stage in the development of a trout, salmon, or char.

SPAWN The mating of fish. Also, a mass of fish eggs.

SPAWNING RUN The migration of fish to the place where they mate and lay their eggs.

SPENT The adjective describing a fish or insect after it has deposited its eggs.

SPILLWAY The place where water flows over a dam.

SPINNER The final stage of a mayfly's life cycle, when it mates and the female deposits its eggs on the water.

SPLICE The connection of two pieces of line.

SPLIT SHOT Small balls of heavy metal sliced so an angler can squeeze them onto the leader to make it sink.

SPRING CREEK A stream fed by a subterranean water source.

STEELHEAD A form of rainbow trout that migrates from the stream in which it was born to the sea or to a large lake, and back to its home stream to spawn.

STONEFLIES Aquatic insects that live in well-oxygenated streams and lakes, often among stones. An important food source for fish.

STREAMER A style of fly usually designed to simulate a fish or eel.

STRIKE The moment when a fish bites or when an angler sets the hook into a fish.

STRIKE INDICATOR A piece of buoyant material attached to the leader that bobs or hesitates in the current to signal that a fish has taken the fly beneath the surface.

STRIP To pull line from the reel or to retrieve the fly by pulling line back in short strokes.

STRIPPING GUIDE The first large ring, just above a rod's handle, through which line passes.

STRUCTURE Submerged objects that attract fish by providing cover.

TAILER A device that loops around a fish's tail so an angler may land it.

TAILWATER A stream flowing from a large dam.

TAKE The moment a fish strikes. Also, the euphemism for the catching or the killing of a fish.

TAPER The narrowing of a fly rod, line, or leader.

TERRESTRIALS Such insects as ants, crickets, and beetles, which live on land but sometimes fall upon the water where they become prey for fish. Also, the generic term for artificial flies that simulate land insects.

TIDE The periodic rise and fall of water levels, caused by gravitational forces.

TIPPET The section of a leader tied to the fly.

TIP-TOP The ring or loop at the top end of a rod through which the line flows.

TROLLING A technique for fishing by towing a fly or other lure behind a boat.

TWITCH A bit of motion an angler imparts to a fly by a slight strip of line.

WADERS Waterproof boots, available in three heights: to the angler's hips, waist, or chest.

WADING SHOES Shoes, usually with felt or cleated soles, that an angler wears over stockingfoot waders.

WADING STAFF A walking stick that gives an angler stability while walking through flowing water.

WEED GUARD Stiff monofilament or wire, attached to large artificial flies, that prevents snagging.

WEIGHT-FORWARD A fly-line design in which the heaviest portion of line is very close to the tip.

WET FLY An artificial fly designed to sink and to simulate an aquatic insect.

WIND KNOT A knot in the leader or line caused by a fault in casting.

INDEX

running line, 137

safety pins, 16
salamanders, simulated, 63
salmon, 13, 62, 73, 108, 108*illus.*
salmon flies. *See* stoneflies
saltwater estuaries, 81
sea robins, 111
shad, 73, 109
shade, importance to fish, 80
sharks, 97, 111
shelves, of lakes, 80
shooting heads (fly line), 9
shrimp, 81
side channels, 78
sinking tip, 137
skates, 111
skating, 59, 89, 89*illus.*
skittering, 89, 89*illus.*
slicks, on water surface, 72
sliders, 137
smolt, 137
snakes, danger from, 115
snakes, simulated, 63
snappers, 111
snook, 109
Soft-Hackle flies, 68
specialty taper fly line, 8
Spider (fly), 89
spillways, 137
spinners (mayflies), 55, 56, 137
splashes, on water surface, 68, 69*illus.*
splashing (fly animation technique), 90, 90*illus.*
spotted seatrout, 109
steelhead, 73, 109, 137
stoneflies, 57–58, 58*illus.*, 138
streamers, 4, 16, 138
strike indicators, 14, 15, 138
striped bass, 109–110
stripping guide, 138
submerged structures, 80
sunfish, 2, 73, 110, 110*illus.*
sunglasses, polarized, 13, 30, 65, 66, 112, 136
sunscreen, 113
Surgeon's Knot, 23, 23*illus.*, 24*illus.*, 26–27*illus.*, 28*illus.*

swimming (fly animation technique), 89, 89*illus.*

tackle. *See* fishing gear
tailing, 70, 70*illus.*
tailwater, 138
tarpon, 107, 110, 110*illus.*
thermometers, 14, 65, 72
thunderstorms, 115
tippets, 6–7, 138
    attaching to leaders, 23–24
    changing to eliminate drag, 86
    shock, 137
trolling, 138
trout, 2, 53, 66, 68, 73, 77, 110–111
tuna, 111
two-winged flies, 58–59

waders, 14, 114, 138
wading belts, 14
wading staffs, 14, 138
wakes, caused by fish, 70
weakfish, 111
weed beds, 78, 80
weed guard, 138
weight-forward fly line, 8, 16, 138
wet flies, 3, 16
whitefish, 111
wind knot, 138
Woolly Bugger (fly), 99
Woolly Worm (fly), 105, 118–119, 119*illus.*
worms, simulated, 63